THE BOOK OF PEACE

Waterstone's collection of writing for Refuge

WATERSTONE'S

PUBLISHED IN ASSOCIATION WITH PENGUIN BOOKS

PENGUIN BOOKS

Published by the Penguin Group
Penguin Books Ltd, 27 Wrights Lane, London w8 5tz, England
Penguin Putnam Inc., 375 Hudson Street, New York, New York 10014, USA
Penguin Books Australia Ltd, Ringwood, Victoria, Australia
Penguin Books Canada Ltd, 10 Alcorn Avenue, Toronto, Ontario, Canada m4v 3b2
Penguin Books (NZ) Ltd, Private Bag 102902, NSMC, Auckland, New Zealand

Penguin Books Ltd, Registered Offices: Harmondsworth, Middlesex, England

First published 1999
1 3 5 7 9 10 8 6 4 2

Set in 10/13pt Monotype Columbus
Typeset by Rowland Phototypesetting Ltd,
Bury St Edmunds, Suffolk
Printed in England by Clays Ltd, St Ives plc

THE BOOK OF PEACE

All proceeds from the sale of this book go directly to Refuge

A national lifeline for women and children
experiencing domestic violence

INTRODUCTION

For twenty-eight years, Refuge has supported women and children experiencing domestic violence. Developing from its beginnings in West London, the world's first refuge, the charity has become a national lifeline for tens of thousands of women and children experiencing domestic violence across the UK.

Domestic violence involves the repeated, habitual and random use of physical aggression or emotional abuse to force a woman to submit to her partner's demands. One woman in nine is severely beaten by her partner each year, and one woman in four has experienced physical abuse from her partner.

Refuge's 24-hour National Crisis Line provides support, advice and, where required, referral to refuges throughout the UK. Refuge offers a place of safety, one-to-one counselling and, vitally, support and practical help when a woman feels ready to leave the refuge. Refuge also runs a unique Children's Programme working with children affected by witnessing domestic violence.

Sandra Horley, Chief Executive of Refuge, is frequently called upon to advise and undertake research for government bodies in the UK and abroad. She has given expert testimony in criminal and civil trials. She has recently been awarded an OBE for her services to women experiencing domestic violence.

Refuge saves lives and helps empower women to rebuild their lives and those of their children; with more resources they could help more women and children look forward to a future free from violence.

CONTENTS

SIMON WINCHESTER

·

The Dubrovnik Peace Project

I met a Swedish mathematician named Jan Suurkula by chance at an airport, and although he knew nothing about me nor why I was in Dubrovnik in the first place, he proceeded to tell me in some detail his particular interest in (a) the unified field theory and (b) its connections, if properly harnessed, with the lessening of human chaos. Since there was a very great deal of chaos in the area just now, he said, you would surely be interested in anything that might lessen it?

His basic thesis was easily stated, though hardly simple. Proving the unified field theory, the notion that all the main forces of physics – electro-magnetism, time, space and gravity – are somehow linked together in a kind of all-encompassing multi-dimensional geometry, has been the Holy Grail of great scientific thinkers for most of this century. That human beings might somehow contribute to, or somehow affect, the frail gossamer threads that link all these physical elements together is what mathematicians like Dr Suurkula have come to believe.

He and his similarly minded colleagues, of whom he said there were *many thousands in almost every country in the world*, were now working to make sure that human interaction with these forces was channelled for the good of all humanity – and, quite specifically, that humans could control their own destiny by harnessing forces within themselves to mitigate the chaos-tending forces of physics. That some humans, in other words, had the power to reduce chaos.

'And to stop war,' he said brightly. 'You are, of course, here for the Congress.'

I said that I had not the faintest idea what he was talking about.

'The Croatian peace conference. Perhaps the most important conference going on in the world today. You are not attending?' he said, incredulous. 'We are on the brink – the very brink, you know – of bringing about peace in the Balkans. There are 200 of us here just now. We only need a few more people. This why I am coming down from Sweden. People are coming in from all over. America. Italy. England. South Africa. We need just a total of, let me see –' he took out a chewed pen and scribbled a quick calculation on the palm of his hand '– 254 people. Once we have them all assembled in one room, then peace will happen. I assure you. It always works.'

I must have looked more than a little mystified, for he sat down beside me and with an accomplished bedside manner began to explain. These, it is important to say, are Dr Suurkula's words, not mine. No product endorsement here. Just mystification and, because of one singular fact that was to emerge later on, a degree of impressed acceptance.

People, Dr Suurkula said, can learn the secret of channelling their internal energies in a way that will communicate vibrations that will, or may, interact with all those inevitable webs that link the various fields of a unified physical geometry. The secret to making that intersection useful, to allow people to make, by way of their mental powers alone, a measurable electronic effect on the way the physical world works, is to gather together a certain critical number of people so that, just like the critical mass in an atomic pile or a bomb, their presence and common effort create a kind of mentally powered fission.

I blinked in disbelief, but the strangely beguiling Dr Suurkula went on. I asked a question: how many people might be needed to make up this so-called critical mass? He was, it turned out, just coming to that.

The number of people required to have a measurable effect on a population varies directly with the size of the population that needs to be affected. Measurements made over the last thirty years, in a variety of towns and cities and countries around the world, had shown incontrovertibly that, by chance – or, in fact, probably not by chance – a perfect mathematical device invariably comes into play. For the critical mass seems always to be reached when the number of people assembled in one place, and all of them manifesting the same vibrations at the same time, is equal to the square root of 1 per cent of the population that is to be affected.

This curiously satisfying mathematical coincidence was noticed first of all in the mid-seventies, in the city of Providence, Rhode Island. The town used to be a wayward place, the car-thief capital of America, a place of murder and burglary and enough crime to make the local police chief throw up his hands in despair. But then Dr Suurkula's friends – people whose names are familiar within this world, John Hagelin, Matti Pitkanen, Neil Phillips, Paolo Menoni – decided to become involved, trying to see if they could direct the powers they believed they had, in a way that they thought might help. They assembled enough of their like-minded colleagues until they had reached the number that equalled the square root of 1 per cent of the Providence population – which, since it stood at 160,000, was the neat and precise number of forty – and put them in a local hotel room and then . . . well, Dr Suurkula said, that was the part that a rationalist, as he assumed me to be, might well choose not to believe.

Too true, I retorted. I had not believed too much of what I had heard so far. Fair enough, he replied, and continued anyway. What these forty people in Providence then did, he said, was to indulge in several powerful minutes of *simultaneous yogic flying*.

Of course, *transcendental meditation*. I might have known. My cynicism went into immediate overdrive. These people, I said to myself, were *completely nuts*. They were part of a pathetic troupe of disciples of the now fabulously rich and probably totally cynical confidence trickster (as I saw him and his like) known as the Maharishi Mahesh Yogi, who had been the spiritual adviser to some of the Beatles and now lived as a wealthy recluse somewhere near Amsterdam.

They, like so many others I had come across elsewhere over the years, and like the disciples of the Baghwan Rajneesh and Sai Baba and a woman called Maya whom half of social Hong Kong seemed to be following, had been gulled into handing over huge sums of their own savings to be taught the nonsense that mental-energies-can-be-harnessed-and-made-to-bring-about-universal-peace, and were now performing in the Balkans, of all places, the same stupefying rituals – which culminated in something so perfectly silly, not to say unattractive, as managing to lift for several continuous seconds their backsides off cushions while sitting in the lotus position – that had made them a global laughing-stock. And they were here trying to persuade innocents like me that by such madness lay the road to peace, that I might perhaps join them, or give them money, or write laudable things and so help them to win ever more credibility. The exploiting of such a tragedy as this – it was all too shabby, too cynical, too tasteless.

Dr Suurkula clearly saw the anticipated doubt on my face and tried to dispel it with a barrage of statistics. The forty people who performed simultaneous yogic flying in Providence, he said, had achieved great success. The number of car-thefts and robberies in the city dropped by 42 per cent over the next week, he said, and has remained lower ever since. Had I heard any further discussion of Providence being the car-stealing capital of America? No, I said, I had not. Well, that was all to do with us! smiled the man, and launched into a barrage of facts and figures.

Look at what we did in Jerusalem in 1979, he said: 230 people – the Israeli population is 5.3 million – performed yogic flying on the eve of the Camp David talks, and a peace agreement was signed. Then again, and most ambitiously, 7,000 people met and performed the rituals in a gymnasium outside Washington, DC, and, their power being harnessed to improve the lot of the then 4.9 million people of the planet, the Cold War ended, the Berlin Wall fell and the atomic stalemate which had dogged the global population for half a century was ended.

His conversation then veered into areas I could not possibly understand – the nature of the five sub-atomic particles, the coincidence of the five levels of Vedic-inspired consciousness, the overlapping circles of energy, the works of Niels Bohr and Erwin Schrödinger and Albert Einstein, the role of the mantra in stimulating internal vibration. And then, on the verge of losing me, he wondered whether I might not come down to the Congress and see the preparations under way to bring peace to the Balkans.

The Dubrovnik Peace Project was being held in an airy resort hotel, the Mincenta, at the north end of town. There were no tourists in sight, just scores of the earnest-looking and friendly people – Germans, Israelis, Britons, Italians, Americans – who were delegates to the conference, and who seemed to spend much of their time languidly strolling from workshop to workshop, or intently reading the messages (for cheap flights home, for organic food shops in town, for phone cards) posted on a bulletin board outside the conference office. It might have been a low-key trade show or a book festival, and the delegates all sales representatives for health-food makers, or sandals. There seemed to be no leaders, as such – just instructors and lecturers, and, once in a while, men who were so well known in the field that the crowds parted before them and emitted a quiet collective gasp of awe.

Dr Paolo Menoni, whose pair of impeccably made business cards pronounced him to be Avvocato and Insegnante di Meditazione Trascendentale, was one such, and he broke off what he was doing – which seemed principally to be talking to a group of excited middle-aged ladies – and sat down to discuss the urgency of the mission, the crisis it had now reached, the need for everyone to come and assemble so that peace might be brought into being.

'You may be sceptical,' he said, 'and I would understand that. But you should know there are now no fewer than fifty-seven proven cases in which what we do – meditating, yogic hopping, skywalking, yogic flying – has truly brought about peace. Read the paper in *The Journal of Conflict Resolution*, back in 1988: it showed without a doubt how this really works. Your William Hague, leader of Mrs Thatcher's Conservatives, he believes in meditation, in the benefits of what we do. So does the President of Mozambique, Dr Chissano. Believe me, this is catching on.'

And Dr Menoni took me through the back of the hotel to what evidently had once been the large socialist-style dining-hall where happy Slavic holidaymakers formerly took their gruel and goulash. In it were hundreds of mattresses, readied for the evening flying session. There was a table on one wall, showing the numbers taking part each day. Two weeks before the numbers had been low: 75, 90, 56. Then, after an appeal went out on the Internet and concerned would-be fliers heard about the critical need to reach the super-radiance number, people started drifting in, and the figures crept up: 130, 178, 203, 217. Now, according to Dr Menoni, there were two figures that were vitally necessary: 254, to stop the war in Croatia and Bosnia, and 345, which was to bring peace to Yugoslavia.

I pointed out that there was actually no war going on in either Croatia or Bosnia, which perplexed him a little. But the figure of 345 was indeed the square root of 11.9 million, which was more or less the population of

Yugoslavia. (More or less: the official figure appears to be 10.59 million.) If perhaps the pleas and telephone calls and telexes that were being sent out from the Mincenta did lure the faithful in sufficient numbers, then perhaps, just perhaps, peace might break out.

I left them just as they were beginning a session. Scores of earnest-looking and very friendly middle-aged men and women – there were few youngsters in the group – were taking off their shoes, signing up for the coming attempt and taking up positions on their various mattresses. An instructor mounted the podium, muttered a few words of Sanskrit by way of universal greeting and told everyone to begin mouthing their mantras. And then another pair of instructors looked at me to suggest I might leave, and drew shut the curtains. As I walked away a low, rhythmic chanting was beginning, a humming and a thumping and the sound of a growing ecstasy. I turned the corner and there was the Adriatic, and in place of human ecstasy the sound of waves crashing on the shore two hundred feet below.

Later, when I returned to America, I asked the editor of the *Journal of Conflict Resolution*, Bruce Russett, if he thought there was any merit in the ideas of Transcendental Meditation and of the Dubrovnik Peace Project – whether there was any sense behind the concept of harmonic vibrations and a super-radiance number and the power to influence unified fields and to bring about peace by means of human electronics. Yale University's Dean Acheson Professor of Political Science, for such was his other title, was acerbic in his reply:

My considered opinion is that what the TM folks are peddling is snake oil. The premise that TM can help its practitioners reduce their own conflicts is reasonable; the premise that it can reduce conflict among nearby non-practitioners is absurd.

It is true that JCR, which I edit, did long ago publish an article by the TM folks purporting to show big effects in the Jerusalem area. Even then I regarded the premise as absurd, but after a lot of internal debate decided that the empirical work should be judged on its own merits, separately from the plausibility of its chief assumption, and let it see daylight. That was in the December 1988 issue. A critic took a stab at demolishing their statistical analysis in the December 1990 issue, but in my judgement just missed driving his stake through the heart.

Nonetheless, I have seen nothing since that persuades me that they have any general capability to do what they say; to the degree their Jerusalem experience does fit it is almost certainly a lucky coincidence, and they don't tell us about the tries elsewhere that didn't work. I much regret having gone out on a limb for this, and would advise extreme caution to anyone else.

And yet it so happens that the week during which Dr Menoni was calling for new volunteers – the first week of June, the week when Dr Suurkula arrived at the Mincenta Hotel, the week during which the number of those performing their various yogic feats was climbing up into the one hundreds and two hundreds – there were also significant moves towards peace being made in Belgrade, Moscow, London, Brussels, New York and Washington, DC.

And on *the very day* that the group did manage to assemble 345 yogic fliers, Slobodan Milosevic *did* accept the peace proposals from NATO. Peace of a sort was beginning to break out in the Balkans at precisely the moment that the Dubrovnik Peace Project was working at its hardest and most sustained – when, as its leaders would claim, the vibrational forces were working at their maximum.

Maybe it is all absurd. Maybe what happened in the Balkans, like whatever happened in Jerusalem, can be dismissed as a lucky coincidence. Maybe there are those in the various great churches around the world who believe that their particular prayers or other spiritual intercessions did the necessary. The possibility that man, harnessing some kind of invisible and indefinable energy, can on occasion influence external affairs with which he has no physical connection – the idea intrigues, and remains intriguing, long after the absurdity of the performance has vanished into memory. There is just a faint and lingering thought from Dubrovnik that says, all too quietly – well, *why not*?

From *The Fracture Zone* by Simon Winchester, published by Viking.

MARIAN KEYES

..

The Press Launch and the Rules of Engagement

Daily, invitations to press launches arrived in the post – everything from new lines in eye-shadow to openings of shops – and Lisa and Mercedes ruthlessly shared them out between them. Lisa, as editor, got first refusal. But Mercedes, as fashion and beauty editor, had to be allowed to go to a fair few too. Annie, Cinderella-like, stayed behind to mind the shop, and Trix was way too far down the feeding chain to ever stand a chance of going.

'What happens at a publicity do?' Trix asked Lisa.

'You stand around with a bunch of other journalists and a few celebrities,' Lisa said. 'You talk to anyone important, you listen to the presentation.'

'Tell me about this one you're going to today.'

A shop called Morocco was opening its first Irish branch. Lisa couldn't have cared less. It had been open for years in London, but the Irish franchise holder was treating it as a big deal. Tara Palmer-Tomkinson was flying over from London for the launch, which was being held in the Royalton-inspired splendour of the Fitzwilliam Hotel.

'Will they have food?' Trix asked.

'There's usually something. Canapés. Champagne.'

In fact, Lisa dearly hoped there would be food because she'd started a new eating plan – instead of the Seven Dwarfs diet she'd moved on to the Publicity diet. She could eat and drink what she liked, *but only at publicity events*. Lisa knew the importance of being thin, but she refused to be a traditional diet slave. Instead she incorporated unusual limitations and rewards into her relationship with food, always keeping the challenge fresh and interesting.

'Champagne!' Excitement made Trix Don-Corleone-hoarse.

'That's if they're not a low-rent outfit, and if they are they don't get a plug in the mag. Then you get your goody bag and leave.'

'A *goody* bag!' Trix lit up at the mention of something free. Something that she didn't have to go to the trouble of stealing. 'What kind of goody bag?'

'Depends.' Lisa pouted jadedly. 'With a cosmetic company you usually get a selection of this season's make-up.'

Trix squeaked with delight.

'With a shop like this, perhaps a bag –'

'A bag!' She hadn't had a free bag in *years*, not since they'd started electronically tagging them.

'Or a top.'

'Oh my God.' Trix jigged in excitement. 'You're so lucky!'

After a long, thoughtful pause, Trix suggested, over-innocently, 'You know, you should really take Annie along with you.' The pecking order was such that there was no chance Trix would ever be allowed to go until Annie was. 'She's your deputy editor. She should know what the drill is if you ever get sick.'

'But . . .' Mercedes' smooth olive face was anxious at the suggestion of someone else muscling in on such sacred ground. There were only so many free lipsticks to go round.

Mercedes' palpable anxiety, coupled with the residue of guilt around Annie, made Lisa's decision easy. 'Good idea, Trix. OK, Annie, you can ride shotgun with me this afternoon. That is,' she added disingenuously, 'if you'd like to come.'

Annie had always been bad at holding a grudge. Especially when there was free stuff involved. 'Would I like to come?' She disappointed herself by exclaiming shrilly, 'I'd *love* to come.'

Lisa had lunch at the Clarence with a best-selling author whom she was trying to persuade to write a regular column. It was a success. Not only did the woman agree to do the column for a knock-down fee in exchange for regular plugs for her book, but Lisa escaped the lunch almost unscathed. Despite swirling her food energetically around her plate, all she ate was half a cherry tomato and a forkful of corn-fed chicken.

She returned to work triumphant and was trawling through her mail when Annie showed up beside her desk, with her bag and coat.

'Lisa,' Annie said anxiously. 'It's two-thirty and the invite is for three. Should we go?'

Lisa laughed in sardonic surprise. 'Rule number one – never be on time. Everyone knows that! You're too important.'

'Am I?'

'Pretend.' Lisa returned to her pile of press releases. But after a while she found herself looking up and saw that Annie's avid eyes were fastened on to her.

'For pity's sake!' Lisa exclaimed, bitterly regretting ever inviting Annie.

'Sorry. I'm just afraid everything will be gone.'

'What everything?'

'The canapés, the goody bags.'

'I'm not leaving until three, and don't ask me again.'

At three fifteen, Lisa reached under her desk for her Miu Miu tote, and said to a quivering Annie, 'Come on, then!'

As they made their way to the Fitzwilliam Hotel, the day was chilly and blustery, the mini-heatwave of the previous week but a distant memory.

'One leg-wax doesn't make a summer,' Annie thought sadly, back to wearing trousers again after a long summer skirt had enjoyed a too-brief airing the day before. Then she forgot the weather and ecstatically elbowed Lisa. 'Look! It's your woman, Tara Palmtree-Yokiemedoodle.'

And indeed it *was* Tara Palmtree-Yokiemedoodle, parading up and down on the pavement outside the hotel, surrounded by a throng of frantically clicking photographers.

'Givvus a bit of leg there, good girl, Tara,' they urged.

Annie headed for the road, to walk around the ring of photographers, but Lisa marched determinedly into the thick of them.

'Oi, who are those two?' Annie heard, and tried to squirm away from Lisa. But Lisa's grip on her arm was vice-like.

Then, to Annie's great surprise, Lisa announced, 'Taaaaraaaaa, darling, long time no see,' wrestled Tara into a reluctant air-snog, then swivelled them both to face the cameras. The photographers froze from their incessant clicking, then took in the golden, caramel-haired girl, cheek-to-cheek with Tara, and commenced their clicking with renewed fervour.

'Lisa Edwards, editor-in-chief, *Colleen* magazine,' Lisa moved amongst the photographers, informing them. 'Lisa Edwards. Lisa Edwards. I'm an old friend of Tara's.'

'How do you know Tara Palmtree?' Annie asked, in awe, when Lisa returned to her on the sidelines, where she'd been completely ignored by the photographers.

'I don't.' Lisa surprised her with a grin. 'But rule number two – never let the truth stand in the way of a good story.'

Lisa swept into the hotel, Annie trotting behind her. Two handsome young men came forward, greeted them and relieved Annie of her jacket. But Lisa airily refused to relinquish hers.

'May I remind you of rule number three,' Lisa muttered tetchily, en route to the reception room. 'We *never* leave our jacket. You want to give the impression that you're very busy, just popping in for a few minutes, that you've a far more interesting life going on out there.'

'Sorry,' Annie said humbly. 'I didn't realize.'

Into the party room, where a see-through-skinny woman dressed head-to-toe in Morocco's summer collection established who they were and made them sign a visitor's book. Lisa scribbled a perfunctory few words, then handed the pen to Annie, who beamed with delight. 'Me too?' She squeaked.

Lisa pursed her lips and shook her head in warning. *Calm down!*

'Sorry,' Annie whispered, but couldn't help taking great care as she wrote neatly, 'Annie Kennedy, Assistant Editor, *Colleen* magazine.' She thought she'd burst with pleasure.

Lisa ran a French-manicured nail down the list of names. 'Rule number four, as you know,' she advised. 'Look at the book. See who's here.'

'So we know who to meet.' Annie understood.

Lisa looked at her as if she was mad. 'No! So we know who to avoid!'

'And who should we avoid?'

With contempt, Lisa surveyed the room, full of liggers from rival magazines. 'Just about everyone.'

But Annie should have known all this – and it had just become clear to

Lisa that she hadn't even a grasp of the basics. In high alarm, she whispered, 'Don't tell me you've never been to a publicity bash before? What about when you were with *Woman's Place*?'

'We didn't get many invites,' Annie apologized. 'Certainly nothing as glamorous as this. I suppose our readership was too old. And when we *did* get invited to the launch of a new colostomy bag or sheltered housing project or whatever, Sally Healy was nearly always the one who got to go.'

What Annie didn't add was that Sally Healy was a round, mumsy type, who was friendly to everyone. She had none of Lisa's hard, lacquered rivalry or strange, aggressive rules.

'See him over there?' Awestruck, Annie indicated a tall, Ken-doll-type man. 'He's Marty Hunter, a television presenter.'

'*Déjà vu*,' Lisa snorted. 'He was at the Bailey's bash yesterday and the MaxMara one on Monday.'

This plunged Annie into a distressed silence. She'd had high hopes for this do. She'd wanted to shepherd and mind Lisa and prove to her that she needed her. And she'd anticipated that she'd win some much-coveted respect from Lisa by her indispensable insider knowledge on famous Irish people – knowledge that Lisa, as an Englishwoman, couldn't possibly hope to possess. But Lisa was miles ahead of her, already had a handle on the celebrity situation and seemed irritated by Annie's amateurish attempts to help.

A roaming waitress stopped and thrust a tray at them. The food was Moroccan-themed: cous-cous, merguez sausages, lamb canapés. The drink, surprisingly, was vodka. Not very Moroccan, but Lisa didn't care. She ate what she could, but couldn't go berserk, because she was constantly talking to people, Annie trailing in her wake. Energetically, charmingly, Lisa worked the room like a pro – although it delivered few surprises.

'Same old, same old,' she sighed to Annie. 'The Irish Liggerati – most of these sad losers would show up at the opening of a can of beans. Which brings me smoothly to rule five: use the fact that you still have your jacket as an excuse to escape. When someone becomes that smidgeon *too* boring, you can say you have to go to the cloakroom.'

Wandering around the room were a few doe-eyed models, their unformed, unripe bodies dressed by Morocco. Now and again a PR girl shunted one of them in front of Annie and Lisa, who were expected to ooh and aah about the clothes. Annie, hot with embarrassment, did her best, but Lisa barely looked.

'It could be worse,' she confided, after another adolescent jerked and twisted in front of them, then departed. 'At least it's not swimwear. That happened at a sit-down dinner in London – trying to eat my meal while six girls stuck their bums and boobs into my plate. Ugh.'

Then she told Annie what Annie was beginning to realize anyway. 'Rule number – what are we up to now? six? – there's no such thing as a free anything. Come to something like this and you have to endure the hard sell. Oh no, there's that creepy bloke from the *Sunday Times*. Let's move over here.'

Annie became more and more diminished by Lisa's encyclopaedic knowledge of almost everyone in the room. She'd been living in Ireland less than two weeks and already it seemed she'd bonded with – and dismissed – most of Who's Who.

With her stapled-on smile securely in place, Lisa swivelled discreetly on her Robert Clegerie heel. Had she missed anyone? Then she spotted a pretty young man, squirming uncomfortably in a too new-looking suit.

'Who's he?' she asked, but Annie had no idea. 'Let's find out, shall we?'

'How?'

'We'll ask him.' Lisa seemed amused at Annie's shock.

Assuming a wide smile and twinkling eyes, Lisa descended on the boy, Annie tagging behind. Up close he had spots on his youthful chin.

'Lisa Edwards, *Colleen* magazine.' She extended her smooth, tanned hand.

'Shane Dockery.' He ran a miserable finger under his tight shirt collar.

'From Laddz,' Lisa finished for him.

'Have you heard of us?' he exclaimed. No one else at this bash had a clue who he was.

'Of course,' Lisa had seen a tiny mention of them in one of the Sunday papers and had jotted down their names, along with all other names that she thought she should know. 'You're the new boy band. Going to be bigger than Take That ever were.'

'Thanks,' he gulped, with the enthusiasm of the as-yet-unestablished.

Perhaps it had been worth getting togged out in these terrible clothes after all.

As they moved away, Lisa murmured, 'See? Just remember, they're more frightened of you than you are of them.'

Annie nodded thoughtfully and Lisa commended herself on her kind patronage. Helped, probably, by the copious quantities of vodka she was shipping. Speaking of which . . . ? Instantly a waitress appeared at her side.

'Vodka is the new water.' Lisa raised her glass to Annie.

When Lisa had eaten and drunk her fill, it was time to leave.

'Bye.' Lisa wafted past the stick-insect on the door.

'Thank you,' Annie smiled. 'The clothes were lovely and I'm sure *Colleen* readers will love themmmm!' Annie's sentence ended in a gasp as someone pinched her arm very, very hard. Lisa.

'Thank you for coming.' Stick-insect pressed a plastic-wrapped parcel into Lisa's hands. 'And please accept this little goodwill gesture.'

'Oh, thanks,' Lisa said vaguely, trailing away.

Then one was pressed into Annie's eager hands. Her face aglow, she dug her nail into the plastic to tear it open. Then gasped anew as someone pinched her arm again.

'Oh, er, yeah, like, thanks.' She tried and failed to sound casual.

'Don't touch it,' Lisa muttered, as they strolled across the lobby to collect Annie's jacket. 'Don't even look at it. And never, *ever* tell a PR girl that you'll give them coverage. Play hard to get!'

'Rule number seven, I suppose,' Annie said sulkily.

'That's right.'

After they'd left the hotel, Annie flicked Lisa an inquiring look, then glanced at her present.

'Not yet!' Lisa insisted.

'When, then?'

'When we get around the corner. But no hurrying!' Lisa upbraided, as Annie almost started to run.

The minute they were round the corner, Lisa said, 'Now!' And they both tore the plastic off their parcels. It was a T-shirt, with *Morocco* emblazoned across the front.

'A T-shirt!' Lisa spat in disgust.

'I think it's beautiful,' Annie said. 'What will you do with yours?'

'Bring it back to the shop. Change it for something decent.'

The following day both the *Irish Times* and the *Evening Herald* ran a front-page picture of the Tara and Lisa clinch.

Marian Keyes's most recent novel, *Last Chance Saloon*, is published by Michael Joseph. 'The Press Launch and the Rules of Engagement' is an extract from her current novel in progress.

MARTYN BEDFORD

...

Attaining the VIZ

Duncan headed for a vacant table, talking all the while on his mobile. *No, Malcolm . . . no, not an option. Nicht eine optione . . .* The phone was black and slim and looked, to Louisa, as if it could be snapped in two as easily as an after-dinner mint. She followed him, carrying the tray with deliberate care, visualizing herself reaching the table without dropping everything. Almost there. Duncan was already seated. He had propped his briefcase on the adjacent chair and slipped out of his suit jacket without once letting go of the phone or interrupting the conversation. She set the tray down. The cafeteria spanned the motorway, columns of traffic overlooked by plate-glass picture windows ranged along one wall. Their table was directly above the fast lane of the southbound carriageway. No noise reached them, though now and then the glazing would vibrate in imitation of a wasp trapped in a jam jar. She tried not to look out. *Malc, mate, I'm losing you.* The seats were fixed to the floor and to each other and to the table, and the table was bolted to the floor. Item by item, Louisa transferred the contents of the tray on to the table.

Duncan swore and shut off the mobile. He helped himself to a cafetière, cup, saucer, spoon, sugar sachets, two small milk cartons and a Danish pastry. The table was wet. Louisa swabbed it with a paper napkin, then used another on her hands. She smelled her fingers: tea. A cold, stewed odour that reminded her of school dinners, although she didn't recall them serving tea at her school. Sitting opposite him, she shrugged the jacket from her shoulders so that it draped over the seat-back. The place was busy, tinny with overlapping talk, muzak and a percussion of crockery and cutlery. Beneath them, the motorway played like a film with the soundtrack erased.

'What is it with these things?' Duncan said.

Louisa watched him pick at the foil seal. His nails were blunt, chewed. She hadn't noticed this about him before and the discovery was intimate and slightly shocking. Her gaze snagged at the ends of his fingers as it would on a scar or some anatomical deformity.

'Here, let me.' She took the carton, snapped-and-peeled and tipped the milk into his cup. She did the same with the other carton. 'There's a knack, I think.'

He sniffed. 'Basic design flaw.'

As he stirred sugar into the coffee, a cufflink clicked against the edge of the table. His shirt was so blue it dazzled her. He produced a pack of cigarettes and lit up, releasing smoke into the light-fixture suspended overhead.

He offered her one, grinning. 'Go on, you know you want to.'

Louisa shook her head.

'You'll crack. You don't have the willpower.' He set the cigarettes aside, next to the phone, and laid the lighter squarely on top of the pack. 'Fifteen quid a week, I spend on fags.'

'Yeah, I reckon I used to . . .'

'Seven hundred and eighty a year.' Duncan, cigarette wedged in the V of his fingers, broke off a piece of pastry and placed it in his mouth. Chewing, he added, 'Criminal, when you think about it.'

They ate. Louisa was hungry, she'd skipped breakfast because of the early start and now it was almost twelve. Tired, too. She suppressed a yawn. Her pastry was stale, pock-marked from where the icing had adhered in gluey clots to the cellophane wrapping. She tried not to eat with conspicuous haste, measuring out each bite between sips of scalding tea. Duncan inspected his watch.

'Geneva are calling at half-twelve, GMT, so we ought to get cracking.' He removed a document from his briefcase and made space for it. 'Now then.'

In an ideal world they would have received an advance copy each, he said, but there hadn't been time. As per. So what they'd do was just rattle through this one together. He drummed the form with a Biro. She found herself nodding, as though his pen was tugging her chin up and down on an invisible thread. The dark hairs on the backs of Duncan's fingers were so neat they might have been combed.

'Any problems with that?'

'No.'

'You know, cos the VIZies were agreed last time and the Specified Targets are . . . well, either they've been attained or they haven't. Figureswise.' He spread his hands. 'Consensus?'

It had been a year since the previous appraisal, and she couldn't recall what VIZ stood for. Something something zones. Virtual? *Vital.* Vital Improvement Zones, that was it. Louisa leaned forward, sitting awkwardly so that she didn't have to read upside-down. Her VIZies were wordprocessed in precise tabulation. Sales. Technical Knowledge. Teamwork. Time Management. Output. Budget. Career Development. Personal Development. She didn't remember there being so many.

Duncan was the more resonant. Each remark, each terse analysis of her performance punctured the air, gathering the glances of other diners. Louisa was aware of mumbling her responses, as if speaking in an undertone might cause him to moderate his own voice. It struck her that they could be mistaken for lovers quarrelling in public: one strident, oblivious to the spectacle they created; the other, seized with self-consciousness. Duncan, as lover, wasn't something she wanted to think about.

'See, I'm looking at twelve months' work here, Louisa, and I'm getting . . . three months' worth of progress. Four, tops.' He spread his hands again. 'And what I'm saying is, are we operating on different satisfaction thresholds?'

'No, it's just –' she inhaled through her nose – 'I suppose it depends how you quantify, I mean . . . how quantifiable these things are.'

Duncan looked at her. He repeated the word 'quantifiable' to himself, in the way that a cat investigates a piece of food before deciding whether to eat it.

It was soporifically warm, their table – finished in shiny yellow Formica – was drenched in sunlight. She wanted to pick up the appraisal document and fan herself with it. As they talked, as *he* talked, she fretted at her necklace, running a finger back and forth in the thin loops of links. There was a sudden commotion at the next table: a child had knocked over a beaker and was being scolded by his mother. Louisa studied the boy's face. Four years old, maybe five. She resisted a compulsion to go over to the woman and tell her, For God's sake it was an *accident*.

'Louisa.'

'Sorry . . . miles away.'

'Can we?'

'Yeah, sorry.'

He took her through another VIZ, then another. She raised the tea to her lips, trailing drips on her skirt and watching them dissolve into the dark fabric. The skirt was creased from so many hours' driving. Being driven. Duncan's voice reeled her in. He was inquiring after her Time Management skills.

'There was a half hour last Wednesday morning,' she said. 'I think I managed that quite well.'

He didn't smile. 'You want me to add Sense of Humour to the list of VIZies?'

Crushing his cigarette stub in a foil ashtray, he picked up the mobile on the second bar of the theme tune to *The Great Escape. Yeeello . . . Malc, what happened?* She caught a scent of tobacco and spilled orange. The child was crying now, the mother silently staring out of the window as if she might at any moment hurl her son, or herself, into the spool of traffic below. Was that possible? No, the window would be sealed shut, the glass toughened. Triple-glazed, by the looks. Perhaps that was why the tables and chairs were secured, to prevent them being used to smash the windows. *I'm expecting the call at twelve-thirty. Yeah. Nope. See to it, will you? No, I have to keep the line clear.* Duncan finished on the phone and checked the time.

'Where were we?' He frowned at the paperwork. 'Right, yeah. Career Dev.'

He pronounced it Korea. A man across the aisle was observing them, eavesdropping, feigning interest in his paperback. She cleared her throat. 'Couldn't we finish this back at the office?'

Duncan looked up. 'I thought we agreed?'

'Or in the car, even.'

'And that would make a difference to your performance rating?'

She didn't say anything.

'Look, Geneva are due on in ... seventeen minutes. There's nothing here we can't wrap up in seventeen minutes. Eh?' He smiled. 'Good.'

Louisa's fingers were tacky from the Danish pastry. When she wiped them, wafery shreds of serviette stuck to the skin. She plucked the paper off then sucked each finger in turn, and both thumbs. Duncan – igniting another cigarette, eyes shuttered against the fumes – turned the page.

He sleeved the document in a clear plastic wallet, replaced it in the briefcase and snapped the latches shut.

'Anything you'd like to discuss?'

She shook her head.

'Hn?'

'No, I don't think so.'

He nodded, maintaining eye contact for a moment. Louisa looked down at the table. She could have rested her head on folded forearms and fallen asleep right there, among the cups and plates and the glistening dandruff of spilled sugar granules. She imagined the sugar, gritty like sand against her warm flesh. Duncan was talking again.

'Six minutes. Time for a quick visit.'

He eased himself out from the seat and made his way across the cafeteria: the brilliant blue of his shirt, the stride, the reflective flash of the door to the gents and its slow, slow closure. The cigarettes, lighter and mobile remained where he had left them; neat slabs among the debris of drinks and cakes. She craved a cigarette. She wanted to sit there and smoke his cigarettes one after another. At the next table, the boy was being readied to leave. Catching the mother's eyes, Louisa smiled, but the woman's expression hardened against her. She exuded an air of fatigue the accumulation of which could only be guessed at.

Louisa yawned. *The objective, Louisa, is to develop a culture – a corporate and individual culture – of achievement.* The emphasis had been on the word 'individual'. She smiled to herself. There was to be another appraisal, in four months instead of twelve. Which was fine. Which was better than she had expected. Her gaze drifted to the motorway. Perched, motionless, above the zip-zip-zip of colour, the sheer velocity, the tumult, it was impossible to believe that a series of white lines could effect such a fluke of integration. She closed her eyes and took several deep breaths; when she opened them again she was staring at Duncan's cigarettes. He was right, it was a question of willpower. The power of will.

The door to the gents was still closed. He would return at any moment, in time for the call, and she would listen to his share of the conversation, in French, and be impressed by it. Then they would retrace their steps to the car and he would drive them to the next meeting. Geneva sewn up. The air-con would be on in the car. He would use the mobile and she would use the laptop as best she could, given the glare and the motion of the vehicle and her preoccupations. Sometime tomorrow they'd be back at the office, her appraisal – incorporating his annotations – to be retyped for signature, in duplicate, and filing. She would be handed her copy. Louisa went to massage her eyes but stopped herself, on account of the make-up. She looked at the door to the gents.

The thought must have occurred first, even fractionally, but the deed was so immediate and unhesitating as to seem to her to be simultaneous with, and indivisible from, the notion that prompted it. A reflex. Reaching across the table, she picked up Duncan's mobile phone – it was even lighter, less substantial, than she'd anticipated – raised the lid of the stainless-steel pot of boiled water that accompanied the tea and slipped the phone in soundlessly and without a splash. There. Easy as that. The mobile, pearled with bubbles, lay flat and black on the bottom like a dead fish. A residue of steam lifted from the pot, moistening her face as she peered down at what she had done. She let the lid fall shut. She thought her hands would be tremulous, but they weren't. They were steady. They were dry and steady. Louisa stood up and went to Duncan's jacket, still shrouding the seat-back. She removed the bunched keys and fob for the electronic alarm, transferred them to the pocket of her own jacket, put the jacket on and walked away from the table, down the stairs and out into the parking area. In the fresh air, the strength of the sunshine felt benign. A cool warmth, if that wasn't a contradiction. Her shoes clicked on the asphalt. The seat would need adjusting, as well as the rearview mirror, and she'd have to ease up to the biting point of an unfamiliar clutch. But a car was a car. And, as Louisa deciphered the glimmering ranks before her, the wine-red torso of the company Lexus looked about as unexceptional as a vehicle could look. She reached for the keys.

Martyn Bedford's third novel, *The Houdini Girl*, is published by Viking.

EDITH VELMANS

....

Good Neighbours

It is awkward to stand there by the window, holding the curtains in such a way that no one can see her from outside. Her eyes are focused on the street, trying to distinguish the faces of the cluster of men having a heated discussion together and slapping each other on the back. Now and then one of them looks up; it seems to her that his glance touches the roof of the house sheltering her. It is dark in her room; because of the blackout no light is allowed to be seen outside. She has to be careful not to lose her balance on the wobbly old stool that helps her reach the window.

Dusk is settling on the village. She wonders why these farmers, usually so stern, are so excited. She knows their faces. She knows that they are 'good'. Each one of the farmers in this village is hiding someone like her, a fugitive, resistance fighters and Jews, people whose lives are in danger.

Tante Bep, her foster-mother, told her that when the Nazis made it impossible for the Jews of Holland to go on living a normal life, the vicar of the only church in the village had urged all his parishioners to open their homes to those who were persecuted. Tante Bep told Erica that there was only one farmer, Farmer Teun, who had refused to take the risk.

Therefore, Teun is not 'good' like the others. 'Good' are those who dare to resist the occupiers, thereby risking their own lives. 'Bad' are those who are profiting from the German occupation or are the enemy's voluntary helpers or are simply too weak to defy the Nazis and whose fear leads them to betraying people whose lives are in danger. That's how Tante Bep puts it. Her voice, usually soft and gentle when she speaks to her foster-child, is stern and disapproving.

Nobody speaks to Farmer Teun now. Tante Bep, like most of the villagers, even turns her back on him when he approaches her in the street. Erica would hate to deserve Tante Bep's disapproval. She always does her best to behave, because these good people are hiding her in order to save her life. And if she doesn't behave, who knows what will happen? She has to be very careful. That's why she cannot go outside or show herself at the window.

Sometimes when dusk sets in, Oom Jan, her foster-father, allows her to help him work in the barn and feed the cows. She feels safe just being in that barn and breathing in the smell of the animals who do not know anything about her and cannot betray her.

It's funny to think that at the other farms there may be other children hiding, who could play with her if it weren't so dangerous. And dangerous it is, says Oom Jan. That's why she keeps herself busy with chores around the house and tries to concentrate on the lessons Tante Bep gives her.

It has been almost three long years that she hasn't seen her parents. Or heard from them.

'Look outside, Erica!' Tante Bep's voice sounds very excited. She peeps through the curtains again and sees a line of German trucks filled with ragged soldiers, slowly following more troops on bicycles loaded with bags, utensils and packages. Bringing up the rear are other very young soldiers on foot. No more patriotic songs, no goose-steps.

'What's happening?' Erica cries out.

'They say the British and Canadians are pushing through the German lines,' Tante Bep calls back. 'It looks like the Germans are fleeing, they are running away. Soon the war will be over! And we'll be free again!'

Erica has never seen her foster-mother so excited. 'Will there be peace soon?' she asks. 'Will I see my own parents again?'

'Yes, my darling. And then you'll go back to them and you'll have to leave us. I'll miss you terribly.'

Erica does not know what to make of this news. She wants to stay with Tante Bep. She's been here so long she hardly remembers her parents. She can't imagine the war being over. So she takes another look out of her peephole. Many villagers are lined up along the road, watching the fleeing remnants of the once-victorious German army pass by. Nobody utters a word.

Farmer Teun is standing on the other side of the street. Two neighbours are next to him, and when he turns to them to say something, they pointedly turn away and ignore him. Erica cringes, because she knows this is very rude and she feels a little sorry for Farmer Teun, wishing that she could run to him and say: 'Hello, you must be glad this is almost over . . .' But naturally, that's out of the question, because she is still in hiding and the Germans are still here, no matter how defeated they look.

Uncle Jan comes into the room, beaming and rubbing his hands. 'Erica,' he says, 'it's almost over! Did you see that sad lot moving through the streets? They're definitely on their way home. Can you believe it?'

Her mind is a jumble of joy and anxiety. Is the end of this terrible war really in sight? Will this be the end of the fear? What lies ahead? Will she be able to go to school again and do the same things as all the other Dutch children? Will her mother and father come to fetch her or will she stay with Tante Bep and Uncle Jan? So many questions; she finds it difficult to fall asleep.

Early the next morning she wakes to hear Uncle Jan's radio blaring through the house. She never knew he had a radio. He must have hidden it as carefully as he hid her. If the Nazis had found it, he could have been sent to a concentration camp. 'The Allied Divisions are breaking through the German lines. Our enemies are finally withdrawing . . .' She doesn't have to hear another word. She pulls on her clothes and runs downstairs.

Her foster-parents are already in the kitchen when she comes down. 'You can go outside, Erica. The enemy is gone. You don't have to be afraid any more.'

Outside in the street everybody is kissing and hugging. And amongst them, pale but happy like Erica, are other Jews and fugitives. Some farmers had hidden one child, like her own foster-parents; others a married couple, or a downed British pilot. One farmer's wife proudly shows off the little toddler she sheltered. The children dance around wildly. Some of the older people are crying.

Suddenly the street turns quiet and Erica notices that all eyes are directed towards Farmer Teun's house. Teun is standing in front of his door, alone. She asks herself, 'Can't they leave him alone? Must they go on despising him?' He takes off his cap and smiles at his neighbours, who do not smile back. He looks back over his shoulder and nods to someone behind him. Out comes his wife, followed by an old man and woman, both leaning on canes. Then a whole family: a father and mother holding the hands of four children, and a young couple with a baby wrapped in a blanket. Bringing up the rear are four young men. They all blink their eyes in the morning sunlight.

The villagers, mouths wide open, watch the procession approach. Nobody can think of anything to say. Then Farmer Teun speaks up: 'Sorry, friends, I understand what you thought of me. But with fifteen people hiding in my house, I couldn't tell a soul. But that's behind us now. Come, don't look so glum! Let us all thank God and celebrate!'

'Good Neighbours' is based on a true story that took place in the Netherlands during the Second World War, in the little town of Aalten, where 1,200 inhabitants hid some 2,500 people.

Edith's Book by Edith Velmans is published by Penguin.

PATRICK McGRATH

.....

The Taproom

Harry would have gone behind his screen to get dressed. When he emerged, and had donned his hat – a large black tricorn pulled low over his brow, and crowned with glossy black plumage – and his coat of sweeping black velvet, with dark blue frogging, and silver buttons down the front – and a good deal of crafty padding in the back, to emphasize his deformity – he was no longer the man Martha knew. Black stockings under dark blue velvet breeches, and on his feet black leather shoes with stacked heels and silver buckles. He would gaze gravely down at her in all his painted strangeness, and strike a pose, one hand tucked into his coat, the other cocked akimbo on his hip, and ask her how he looked, and if the people downstairs – now loudly anticipating the appearance of a monster – would like him.

Martha loved her father with all the passion of which a young girl is capable, and she never saw him as a monster. Oh, she knew how grotesque he could render himself when he wanted to, for in truth the architecture of his backbone, in the aftermath of its breaking and mending, was of such grandeur, in a certain light, and with padding, that with but the merest touch of theatricality he could make himself quite horrid. But for Martha he was never horrid. She adored her father, and now, harkening, perhaps, to a fiddle below, he extended a tentative foot, made a step or two of a jig – and Martha needed no more invitation than that, for nothing warmed her quicker than a jig. She unpinned her hair and a moment later the pair of them were happily at it, himself all comical gravity as Martha high-stepped it nimbly about his shuffling legs, her skirts lifted in her fingers and her head flung back, her brick-red tresses streaming out behind her! Oh, they had only the faint strains of a distant fiddle to drive their jig, but soon the dust was rising, the old boards groaning beneath their feet – until there came that knock at the door, that wheedling voice – 'Five minutes!' – and they slowed, and stopped, and gazed at each other with shining eyes and deep dismay.

Harry returned to his mirror to repair the damage done by the jig, and Martha drifted to the window, which overlooked the yard and the stables that enclosed it; and as she stood there, idly gazing out, pinning her hair up and humming the tune to which she had just been jigging, she saw a small black carriage with a nobleman's coat-of-arms in flaking gold-leaf on the door, as it came rumbling down the cobbles and into the yard, with a spidery creature all in black up on its cab. The sun was setting, shadows were thickening, the air was warm and close and heavy with the smell of malt. This was the evening Lord Drogo came to the Angel.

Lord Drogo was the first to descend from the carriage. According to my uncle, Martha would not often have seen an Englishman of this stripe before, and never, certainly, at the Angel. I asked him to describe his lordship, and he told me with some circumspection that while Lord Drogo's clothes bore no sign of ostentation, and his wig was modest – the ivory cane 'tactful' – in the marble brow, and superb aquilinity of feature, Martha would have read at once the marks of a high birth and an imperial temper, not to say an intellect of some vigour and cultivation. Drogo glanced about him, said my uncle, and his cold blue eye missed nothing.

A moment later William himself emerged from the carriage. He stepped down, he told me, with a wheeze of self-mockery, with a good deal less decorum than his master had, and in his wake the carriage shuddered violently on its springs. He too looked about him, frowning, and rubbing the back of his neck where two small hard lumps beneath the skin – this memory apparently giving him pause for reflection – had for some time caused him anxiety.

I liked the sound of the Angel, for here was a genuine fragment of mutilated antiquity. Largely constructed in the days of Henry Tudor, over the centuries its beams had shifted and settled to their own comfort rather than the squared elevation of the builder. The slates were shaggy with

weeds and moss, and undulated like a body of water agitated by the wind;
and so streaked and pocked were the bricks and plaster that the walls had
to be constantly caulked, like the hull of a ship, lest they opened to the
elements and the house sank. The effect was one of faltering decreptitude,
the whole thing like an old man's frame, kept upright and alive only by
the animating inward presence of its tenants. And how the tenants did
animate that frame!

In they came through the back door. The taproom was crowded that
night, and oh, it was a hellish place, said my uncle William, with a theatrical
shudder, all heat and smoke and noise, a large, dark, low room with a
flagged stone floor and bowed black beams across the ceiling. It stank, he
said, of uncleanliness and spoilage. Vast mossy kegs with dripping spigots
were stacked on trestles along the wall, and two beefy women in aprons,
Moll Goat and her daughter Sal, moved among the company with barks
and curses, attempting to serve and control the more than seventy customers
milling about down there. They had come for the entertainment, they were
there to see Harry Peake, whose fame by this time extended well beyond
Smithfield, indeed he was almost as famous as Sal Goat, who was known
from Ludgate to the Tower as the tin-toothed trollop with the heart of tin.

William remembers opening the taproom door and gazing with horror
at the scene within, the seething crowd of poets, apprentices, cutpurses,
footpads, strumpets, thieves, butchers, porters, fops and sailors all now
eager for the appearance of Harry. There was a considerable number of
theatre people present, and up at the counter, and drinking hard, stood
several private soldiers in the faded red coats of an infantry regiment, these
men bound for the American colonies and expecting any day to take ship
for Boston, which was then under British military occupation. Deep in
conspiracy at the back of the room, in a dense fog of tobacco smoke, sat
a passel of muttering radicals, and at a table nearby three old printers
wagered farthings racing lice they had picked with inky fingers from one
another's wigs. A few last dusty beams of sunlight came shafting through
the smoke, and a lurid red glow suffused the place and all its patrons.

Lord Drogo, to whom, it was said, nothing human was alien, joined my
uncle in the doorway and lifted an eyebrow at the landlord, a tall, thin
man of vicious aspect who worked steady and watchful behind a broad

wooden counter, and who, alert to the arrival of quality, now came forward wiping his hands on his apron to inquire as to his lordship's pleasure. This was Joseph Goat, and he ruled absolute in the Angel.

Martha did not attend her father's performances. He had told her of the pain it would cause him to think of her watching him as he displayed himself to a paying public, and so she did not. But she did sit on the stairs where she could listen. Darkness would have fallen by now, branches of candles burning fitfully from wall-sconces as voices continued to rise and huge turbulent shadows surged over the walls. At the back of the taproom hung a black curtain that screened off a low platform, and she would hear Ned Lour clamber on to this platform and call for silence. He would then make his introduction, saying that it was his honour – derisive cheering here – to bring before the esteemed company of the Angel that friend of the people, that towering genius, that most remarkable of men, Mr Harry Peake; and more in this vein, as the crowd stamped and whistled and shouted.

Martha would then hear the curtain being drawn back to reveal that the platform contained one piece of furniture only, a great chair covered by a rich-woven cloth of black and red velvet with a tasselled silver fringe trailing on the floor; and in this chair reclined her father, wearing a pair of spectacles, idly perusing a volume of Dryden, and on his face an expression of such comic aristocratic *hauteur* that it brought a howl of recognition from his audience. This crowd had no affection for the peerage.

The laughter would die soon after and there would then be a silence, or rather, more than a silence, a distinct inholding of the breath. For Harry's face was powdered to an unnatural chalky whiteness, and his eyes were blacked with kohl, so they seemed in the candle-flame terrifying caves of darkness, with the merest pinprick of light blazing deep within. It made a haunting spectacle, said William; he seemed something from a dream, or from the realm of the vampires. Much murmuring now, a yelp or two from the dandies present; and then Harry rose to his feet, and turned, and it was at that point that his audience properly saw the shape of his back.

Harry was right to forbid Martha to watch. My uncle described to me what happened next. Harry, still with his back to the audience, threw off his coat and opened his shirt and pushed it off his shoulders, and they all glimpsed in the gloom the strange bony formations, the peaks and ridges that had lifted and skewed his spine, and pushed his shoulders awry, such that the upper torso of what otherwise would have been a strapping frame was as a bent and broken thing; a length of crooked timber.

The effect upon the company was powerful, whispered my uncle. But this, I said, was simply a *disfigured man* – a man with a twisted spine? Ah, but it seems it was more than that. This was a more primitive age than our own, when Nature was celebrated more for her botches than her glories, and Harry Peake's spine, said my uncle, disturbed the people's confidence in the proper shape and form of things, a confidence they had not known they possessed, it was stitched so deep in their sense of the order of the world. There was a collective gasp of horror, said my uncle, and then Harry reclined once more in his chair, lay there in the posture of a weary noble poet before bestirring himself to read a few lines.

But then the sparks would fly, said William. For Harry's voice had matured like old port wine, it was deep and rich and fruity. It was from his own dark epic that he took his readings, and such were the passages chosen, and such the manner in which he spoke them – striding about, now whispering, now thundering, now turning his great back on his audience and peering round it like a man behind a wall – that they might as well have been political tracts, so sharply did he bring them to bear upon the great questions of the day, by which I mean corruption, power, and empire! Its theme was the Fall, its setting the New World, and its hero a poet roused by tyranny to struggle against the intrusion of empire – already, you see, cried the old man, he was thinking on the grand scale! For by this time, of course, the popular outrage at the Crown's assault on the natural rights of the American colonies grew more passionate with every fresh abuse those people suffered.

Imagine the scene, he said. He was excited now. He wished to convey to me what he had come to understand as the particular power that Harry had, when his genius was in full flood. Harry lifts his head (he whispered), he gazes up into the roof, and silence falls. Oh, and then something marvellous happens! The breast heaves and the eyes roll, and Harry's voice is at once filling the room, it is ringing out with a deep masculine music, it is as though this weary humpback has been taken up and possessed by a spirit alien to his own nature! His very back seems to grow straight! Wildly now he chants his verses, and his words arouse before the company's eyes a landscape that they recognize, for it bears resemblance to the hills and woods and rivers of England, but it is an English landscape made immense, made terrifying, made to a scale of greatness, like a boy changed into a giant, or a man into a god! Oh, it is a vision of untamed Nature that will inspire Harry Peake to the end of his days, cried my uncle, the vision of a great river – as yet it had no name – sweeping through a wilderness, through the forests and mountains of a distant continent he had never seen, a vast wild land of infinite and awful grandeur –!

And all the while the audience sat spellbound, all but a few, the radicals, who were watching not Harry but the soldiers, who seemed however more intent upon their drink, and the whores, than the performance; and they in turn were watched by Francis Drogo, who missed nothing, but who reserved his closest scrutiny for Harry Peake.

'The Taproom' is an extract from Patrick McGrath's current work in progress, *Cape Harry* (working title), to be published by Viking in 2000.

HELEN DUNMORE

......

At the Lake

The lake is cold. It doesn't matter how gingerly you go down the ladder, dipping a toe and then a foot, scooping up water to rub your goose-fleshed arms – the moment will come when you have to let go, push off, allow the water to take your body, and take your breath away. And after a few minutes' thrashing, suddenly you can bear it. It doesn't hurt any more. You swim on, kicking hard, nearly used to it now. A trail of bubbles spins out behind you. It's wonderful. You want to turn round and shout to the woman at the top of the ladder: 'It's all right! Come on in, the water's lovely!' But of course she's wary, too. She's seen you wincing and flinching your way in. She's rubbing her own goose-flesh . . .

There are those who never hesitate, even on the coldest days. Down they clamber, step after step. Even as the water closes over them, their expression doesn't change. Off they swim, resolute, cheerful, and perhaps a little smug.

But there are days when even the deepest water slowly warms. True lake days. After a few sticky July nights, and blazing days, the temperature chalked on the board by the entrance to the lake starts to rise up into the seventies. 'It's warm!' people call back as they strike off from the ladder into the deep, silky brown water. 'It's really warm!' Their voices peal with surprise and delight. But the resolute, stern, smug ones frown a little, now that everyone else can plunge in just as easily as they do.

But 'warm' is always relative. 'Warm' at the lake never means the soupy lapping of the waveless Mediterranean. Warm doesn't mean comfort. This is spring-fed water, as deep as legend, filling the ancient depths of a limestone quarry. We're in a country of springs, though we don't know them as well as our ancestors did. There's Bath a dozen miles away, Aquae Sulis, where tired, cold, fed-up Romans must have felt themselves opening up like flowers in the steamy heat. The relief of it, after tramping miles on those bitterly straight roads. There's Hotwells, closer still, once a spa and now forgotten except when steam rises from the river-bend on winter days. But here, where there once was a quarry, the springs were struck, the limestone gash slowly filled, and the life of the lake began.

Swim out into the middle, past the diving-boards and the water lilies, and imagine the water beneath you, going down and down, yards of it. There are patches where the water warms suddenly, patches where it chills. There are rumours of pike, as thick as a man's thigh, toothed like a freshwater shark. This isn't comfortable, chlorinated, blue-tiled transparent water. There is no lifeguard chomping gum, ready to intervene. There's no shallow end for fooling about, no gentle gradations of depth, no inflatables or water-play, no chutes, no concession to the idea that you have to gussy up water to make it fun. There's only water, acres of it, challenging and inviting. Either you swim, or you don't.

If you look down you may see the watery shadow of your own legs. It's easy to imagine that in the touch of the water there is the nudge of a thousand tiny fish. Sometimes the shape of something huge and hoary seems to glide, deep down, on its way to the hole in the bank where it will wait patiently for its prey to pass. This lake is packed with life. Frogs, toads, fish, yellow flags, water lilies, water mint, weed, dragonflies, water-boatmen. Willows grow around it, grass forms itself into shady lawns, trees and shrubs scramble up the steep slopes. It all has the air of having happened by some wonderful accident. The lake chose to fill itself, the flowers to grow, the fish to multiply. Surely nobody ever built those wooden changing-rooms with their coir matting, stripy curtains, and pungent scent of rope and resin stored in the sun of how many summers. Yellow light squeezes itself through chinks in the wood and smears patterns on to the wall. Women dress and undress, hang up dripping swimsuits, comb hair, rub children with towels. Everything has its own rhythm, and seems timeless. The things we say are the same, year after year. The whole place seems caught in a spell of summer.

But of course no spells work by chance. Read the rules. No radios, no alcohol, no topless sunbathing. No changing outside the changing-rooms. No horseplay. No unaccompanied children at the lakeside. No diving, except at designated places. Everyone must take a swimming test before becoming a member of that deep, unpredictable water. The willows are trimmed, the grass mown, flowers planted, the fish stock monitored. It takes great effort to sustain this appearance of effortless pleasure. Like a landscape planned by Capability Brown, the lake imitates nature, but never bows to it. It knows too much about the underside of nature, and the sprawl of human beings. It understands that if they can, human beings will wreck things for themselves. We'll do it every time, given half a chance, hell-bent on making everyone else enjoy our choice of music, our drunken wit, our rubbish and our braying on the mobile.

And so the lake has its guardians, as well as its rules. They keep the gates, and decide who has really left their membership card at home, and who is trying it on. They know all that is to be known about the long history of the lake. They remember its glorious summers, when crowds of would-be members had to be turned away because the list was full from mid-June onwards. They were there on those long, rainy August afternoons when only a few regulars entered the steel-grey, rain-pocked water. They watched the last swim of the season, when yellowing leaves floated on the lake's surface, and the lawns were bare and quiet. They know who has died, who has been born, and who will make a good committee member. They'll tell you the temperature of the water, but, better than that, they'll tell you what it really feels like.

'Thermometer says it's only 66, but it's all right today. Have you got your card?'

They know about the invaders, who breach the fences at the brambled, hidden top of the quarry, slide into the water and swim for nothing. Once I saw a group of young men challenged at the diving-boards for trespassing. They turned and dived, one after another, and took off in a magnificent racing crawl down the length of the lake, to climb out of the water and disappear into the trees. Perhaps they weren't trespassers at all, but members in another life, from another time. Back then, long before the Second World War, the Olympic diving team trained at the lake. There still exists a black-and-white ciné film of those early days, when people who didn't know that they were old-fashioned swam and sauntered and plunged. They were lords of the present moment, who believed that the lake would belong to them for ever.

And so, in a sense, it does. The lake is full of ghosts, half-hidden in the shadow of the willows, or walking out in the midday sun. The men wear striped one-piece bathing-suits, and stride confidently, masculinely, to the edge of the boards. Their hair is slicked back. They look like Scott Fitzgerald on a good day. They swing their arms back, poise, dive into the sparkling water, and disappear. Even if you rub your eyes you won't see them break the surface again. Women in modest bathing-dresses and rubber bathing-caps duck into the changing-rooms, where the shadows swallow them up. If they saw you, they wouldn't believe in you. They believe in their own perfect day, the present in which they are living, before Hitler and Hiroshima. Their bicycles are flung down on the grass, unchained, and when the closing bell rings they'll cycle off up the white, dusty road which won't be tarmacked for years to come. They are here always, even though they scattered and went to war long ago.

Apart from its population of ghosts, the lake has representatives from pretty much all the ages of humanity. The babies come first, blinking in their car-seats, borne along by young parents who are quite sure that having a baby isn't going to change their lives. They're still going to have a good time, meet their friends, lie in the sun. The baby can come too – nothing easier! But strangely enough the parents seem to spend most of their time hovering over this one little baby. They shade it, then decide it is too cold. They put on clothes, then take them off. They slather the baby with sunscreen, and find its sun-hat. Then it begins to cry, and so they pick it up and walk up and down, up and down under the willows, shushing it, offering it drinks and rusks and favourite toys, all of which the baby spits out on to the grass.

Next, there are the hardened families, in their encampments of folding chairs, rugs, cool-bags and parasols. It's never easy to count quite how many children there are. Two or three families have got together. The parents are offhandedly competent with their children, dishing out crisps, sunscreen and tellings-off while remaining deep in conversation, or trying to read that paperback which they bring to the lake each weekend. It lies splayed out on the grass, walked over by ants. There are skinny, tanned, noisy little boys flicking in and out of the water like eels. There are little girls in solemn conversation, sitting in a row on the duck-boards by the water. There is a puppyish eleven-year-old, not quite old enough to go with the teenagers, gazing at the handsome sixteen-year-old who is just about to dive . . .

Next, and most importantly in their own view, there are the teenagers. They know that the lake really belongs to them. They cycle up after school, or stay all day in the holidays, ten or twelve of them huddled together, endlessly talking, parading up and down in the beautiful new bodies they've just been given, and falling in love with one another. Their favourite preening ground is the diving-boards, where they sun themselves, chat, and look down on the lawns like kings and queens.

Later, they will become couples. Suddenly they're not at school any more. College whizzes past. Suddenly they've got jobs, flats, cars. They come late, after work, to meet other couples. They don't know it, but they're just about to turn into that young pair carrying the baby in the pink sun-hat.

There are others, the freest of all, who don't have to follow any script. They've retired, and their children have long left home. They've been coming to the lake for years – perhaps decades. Their skins are deeply tanned, lined, experienced. Even their grandchildren have grown up. They swim an old-fashioned breast-stroke, heads well up, and then sit in the sun, and talk. They know everyone. They watch the fidgety seven-year-olds waiting to go into the lake for the first time, to take their 50-metre test. They're the first to arrive each season, and the last to go. But sometimes, at the beginning of a new season, one of them is no longer there . . .

Every summer there's one perfect day. Often it comes late in the season, made more precious because you know that the holidays will be over soon. You don't always recognize the day for what it is at the time, while you're living it: the one, the essence of summer. But when you look back, you know. The water was perfect. There was only a small shock of coolness when you climbed down the ladder into the water. You didn't shiver. You struck out smoothly, breathing in the rivery sweetness, past the rocks. You turned over and floated on your back, gazing up at the height of the blue sky, then closed your eyes. You sculled gently, keeping yourself afloat, your ears full of water-noise. When you raised your head, you heard the cries of children, the shouts of teenagers on the diving-boards, someone laughing. There was the far-off drone of the city, muffled by green willows.

When you climbed out you didn't need to dry yourself, because the sun was so warm. You lay flat on your towel, face-down, and shut your eyes. Rivulets of water ran off your skin, tickling you. Perhaps you slept. When you were too hot you went back into the water again, or moved under the green tent of the willows. Fronds of green stirred in the breeze, shifting shadows over sunbathing flesh. You stayed all day, until evening came and they rang the closing bell, and then you made your way slowly back to the car, stunned, sated, hungry. You took a last look back at the lake, which was almost all in shadow by this time, its surface smooth as silk, as if no one had ever swum there. You knew that you would come the next day, and the next, and the next. Every day would be just as perfect as this one.

But the next day it's cloudy, and there's a smell of autumn in the air. Soon you're thinking, *Next season . . .* And you know you're addicted. You can't live without the lake.

Members of the lake are fiercely loyal, but secretive. Yes, they'll agree to outsiders, it can be terribly cold. And deep, too. They never know precisely how deep. They repeat the story of the pike. No, there's nowhere to paddle, and there isn't a café. The lake is a cult, the more precious because there are unbelievers. There are rules, and there are also customs. New members watch the old, learning how to make a camp under the willows, where the deck-chairs are kept, where to fill a paddling pool so that toddlers can enjoy their own miniature lakes. They learn the degree of noisy showing-off which will be allowed to their children, and that which will result in censure from the guardians of the lake. They find out about the rare days when members can swim the full length of the lake, deep into the fishermen's territory, and gain certificates for a quarter-mile, a half-mile, a full mile. The lake is always at its iciest on these days. They learn about showings of the antique ciné film, barbecues, committee meetings, the gains and losses of each season, the stalwart toil that permits the dragonflies of summer to flit on the lake's surface.

Some visit the lake once or twice, taken by a friend, and retreat, baffled. They can't see the point of it. Others are hooked. It is their oasis, only a couple of miles from the city centre. Each year, they fill in their membership applications promptly, while there are as yet no leaves on the trees. They know that no places are kept from year to year. A member of fifty years' standing may be refused, if the annual application form is not received by the set date. The lake operates its own democracy. As the days lengthen, people get anxious. 'Have you got your card yet?' they ask one another, in case somehow they've managed to fill in the form wrongly, failed to sign the cheque, or missed the cut-off date. And then reward comes: the little pastel cards, a different colour for each season, adorned by the hideously grinning photo which you'd thought was all right when you sent it in.

You have got your card. It doesn't matter that it's only April, and you've still got the central heating on. It doesn't even matter much if the weather continues poor all summer. There's bound to be one brilliantly hot weekend, somewhere. The card is your liberty. Even when you don't go, there is always the magical possibility of going. When you're sweating in an office at 5.30 you can look at the clock and say to yourself, 'In twenty minutes I could be in the lake.' You imagine yourself walking barefoot on the grass in the evening sun, your city clothes shucked off on the changing-room bench. Your card is a passport to a small country that will be open to you until September. You have become part of its blues and greens.

As the season opens, members of the lake eye each other in post office and supermarket. They are muffled in winter jackets, almost unrecognizable. Have they been to the lake yet? No, surely no one . . . You can't even begin to imagine the temperature of the water, with all that winter stored in it.

But the moment's coming closer. Suddenly, out of nowhere there comes one of those crazily hot May weekends when the M5 jams with cars heading for the coast. But you don't get your map out. Instead, you dig the cool-box out of the loft, and assemble the first picnic of the year. You scrabble for plastic cups, freezer bags, salt – all the paraphernalia that'll come to hand as easy as breathing, once you've got back into the swing. You look for the rug, the straw mats, the sunscreen. The journey's only a mile, but you're going to another world, where it's always summer. The gates are open, the drive bends downwards, dark, shady, inviting, with the bright splash of grass and water beyond. There's the hut, the blackboard, the guardian coming out to check your cards before slowly raising the barrier.

You are at the lake.

Helen Dunmore has published six novels with Viking and Penguin. Her most recent is *With Your Crooked Heart*.

JOHN MORTIMER

....

Wheelchairs

The reason that childhood is such a difficult, often unhappy period of life is that children are too short to take part in the conversation.

Sitting in a wheelchair at parties, your eyes are on the level of crotches. Drinks are held, samozas and cocktail sausages nibbled and gobbled, high above your head. You are a child again because no one stoops to conversation with you. There is laughter, gossip, flirtations in the upper air; in the world of childhood and old age there is isolation among the knees, only an occasional face is lowered, offers a samoza or a scrap of smoked salmon on soggy bread and floats upwards to the grown-up world.

If wheelchair riders are third-class citizens at parties, they are upgraded at airports, moving in triumph past long queues at passport control, getting only a polite pat at the search for weapons, being let on the empty plane first with children travelling alone and other cripples. Claiming a wheelchair for the leg and blind eye has improved my experience of airports 100 per cent, having been pushed by retired businessmen eking out their pensions, students in their gap year or, occasionally, beautiful girls in uniform. Only once did the wheelchair experience turn from a privileged ride to a journey into hell.

It was at Milan airport and I was waiting at the check-in for the athletic beauty who had zipped me past queues on my arrival to take me to the aeroplane home. It was clearly her day off and her place was taken by a malign dwarf, a small and sinister chair-pusher who offered me, with a shrug of contempt, a chair clearly designed for a child. Wedged into it, I found myself with my knees pressing against my ears, being hurtled through the crowds towards a distant room, bleak, airless and windowless, in which a line of wheelchairs, parked against a blank wall, contained the unfortunate, the partially paralysed, stroke victims and the terminally ill being taken away, perhaps, to die in Palermo. Finding a parking spot at the end of this line, my wheelchair Quasimodo put on the brakes and dumped me.

Gasping for air, I struggled to my feet and limped to a bar for a reviving Prosecco. As I drank I heard a final call for the flight to Heathrow. I rejoined the parade of lost souls and at last Quasimodo reappeared and sped me at a kind of uneven gallop to the gate at which the glass doors were now closed. I could see, however, the BA plane on the tarmac, so I struggled to my feet again, only to be pulled back by my driver, who said, 'You can't move. You're blind! Wait for the lorry!'

Then I saw, far away on the other side of the airport, a lorry with a huge crane on its back. It was advancing slowly, remorselessly, towards the glass doors. I'm still trying to forget being pushed on to a platform, being hoisted into the air by the giant crane and delivered, like a bag of concrete, at the doorway of the plane, to the fascinated amusement of the returning package tourists. I'd rather have been at knee level, bored to tears at a drinks party.

'Wheelchairs' is an extract from John Mortimer's current work in progress, *Summer of a Dormouse*, to be published by Viking in autumn 2000.

VIC REEVES

....

From *Sun Boiled Onions*

This guy plays so fast
he set his hand on fire
during a U.N. peace concert.
Thank god for the U.N.
fire extinguishing service, his
fire was doused and peace
was restored once again to
a troubled world. The guitarist
was arrested for halting the
peace process and burnt at
the stake.

The scourge of the good and kind!
The sight that strikes fear into
the hearts of descent men.
The terrible evil, the unspeakable
invention that causes worldwide
misery to agreeable people. ➤
Making honourable hard working
folk run for cover, fleeing
in despair. from the dreadful
item. The sooner the U.N.
realise this and remove it once
and for all from the hands of
rotten men ~~thembetter~~ and replace
it with cotton wool the better.

RONALD BLYTHE

....

From *Out of the Valley*

NIGHT-WALKING

The night-walker. Not an approved activity, but a rewarding one all the
same, whether in towns or country. In either place one has the world to
oneself. In cities the architecture takes on an ethereal gravity and in the
village all occupancy appears on a short lease. Having to slip away early
from the harvest supper to finish a review, I mention that I shall walk.
Apprehension, solicitude. Have I a torch? But the night-walker has night
eyes. A torch would ruin his vision. The lane twists and turns until it comes
to the pair of old railway sleepers which bridge the ditch, by which time
I can see for miles. The horses are paired like statues, and as still. The grass is
wet and scented. I won't wake Duncan and Jean up because they are at the
party, but I hope their dog will remember me as a friend. Their old farmhouse
looks like a fort and their cropped fields have ceased to belong to anybody
and are just earth. A great clump of paradisal flowers bursts from the path into
the moonless light. Red campion. The Suffolk hills roll up from the Stour and
are temptingly scattered with secret woods. Alas, it is only two miles home,
and I am in the mood to night-walk five. 'You can stay out till breakfast –
you're not a child,' says an eccentric voice. But the review. I dawdle the last
distance, making it last like a sucked sweet. The house comes suddenly into
view. I have taken it unawares. It is wide awake in its hollow and dazzlingly
illuminated by a single bulb. It too has slipped ownership as the work-horses
once slipped their traces and I might be running towards it in 1696. 'You –
those people – those to come – how can you own anything at night?' it is
saying. Max, night-walker extraordinary, sees me and shows off joyously,
dashing up a tree and dancing about.

Some years ago I sat in Coleridge's house in Nether Stowey in the very cottage room in which the young poet wrote 'The Rime of the Ancient Mariner' with one hand, so to speak, whilst rocking his son to sleep with the other. The Wordsworths were nearby at Alfoxden and it was the custom of the three to night-walk in the Quantocks. Oh, the scandal! Three folk, and none of them married to each other, out all night! They were composing *Lyrical Ballads* on the hoof. 'The moving Moon went up the sky/And nowhere did abide.' The Old Testament more than once speaks of 'the vision of the night'. Job was an insomniac and couldn't bear the vision of the night – 'Desire not the night'. Just before St Luke's-tide I stood in the enchantingly lit church at Long Melford with the rector Christopher Sansbury and saw what its builders could never have imagined, an interior revealed from without – by floodlights. A glass gallery of medieval grandees as bright as day.

AND ME A CHILD

Seeking a neighbour to chain-saw up my fallen willow, my mind running on today's mechanical conveniences, which is not something it usually does, I am told that this year is the diamond jubilee of – the combine harvester! 'Combine' because it reaps and threshes all at once. This doubling monster was the invention of two Canadian companies, Massey and Harris. It would also cut the ground from under rural existence as countless generations had known it. Combine-harvesters always remind me of the Padstow 'Oss, which emerges from its dark den into the sunlight for one glorious outing once a year. The leaves now thin on the hazels, I can see the great barn in which Duncan's combine lurks like a satiated beast, having in a single week gobbled up every cornfield for miles around.

The autumn light is at its perfection. In Cambridge all is a sumptuous brown-gold, the river, the colleges, the rusty gardens, the interior of St Botolph's, where I have looked in to view a font carved and painted the very year in which George Herbert would have been at work on his poems. Parts of it are honey-gold. Above Trumpington Street the sky is a tumult of gold, as if dawn and sunset had joined forces or entangled. The ashes of a little boy, Leigh James, have just been laid in St Botolph's churchyard amidst the turning shrubs. In his poem 'Baptisme', Herbert wrote:

O let me still
Write thee great God, and me a childe:
Let me be soft and supple to thy will,
Small to myself, to otheres milde . . .

At Wormingford the names given to a dozen or so boys at the font have been carved a yard or two away on the war memorial. They would have harvested in the old way, the last to do so. It is St Edmund's-tide, East Anglia's patron saint, and the warm November sun presents a golden kingdom of low wheat and silver-gilt hedges, fiery motorways and serial wonders sketched by the Stanstead planes. On the way home from Cambridge I call in at his carpet-bedded shrine at Bury, and where the ruins let in a nippy wind, and where the barons took their oath on his altar that they would enforce King John to sign their great charter. Children race from flinty hump to flinty hump in the keen air, their high voices filling the choir. Bury was Beaduric's homestead when the saint was alive, a Saxon farm where one senses through the confusions of time that he had a welcome. A quiet spot to bury a slaughtered young monarch, some fields on the banks of the Lark. The reading for his day is from Stephen's sermon. They would have been of an age. An architectural mountain of stone was cast up over Edmund's body but eventually pulled down by the townsfolk for their garden walls. At this moment autumn fills all the rents and spaces with its golds and scents and old words.

THE REMAKING OF THE CIRCLE

The old towpaths along the river have been restored and we walk without hindrance of blackberry and nettlebeds all the way to Nayland, collaring the dog as we approach Wissington Mill, as it amuses him to put the wind up Suki's peacocks. They squawk in the icy air. Vast cleared ditches are exposed like excavated longboats below the winter wheat. It is quite unbelievably cold and there is a promise of snow on snow. 'No,' says the German friend, 'it is not very cold – quite warm, in fact. In Berlin it is cold. Fifteen under.' We shudder. I think of the farm labourers of my boyhood as they sugar-beeted at New Year, chopping and kicking the roots from the iron ground, picking them up and trimming them with a tool which was part spike, part knife. They wore sacking cowls, like monks, and leather mittens, and they toiled in sociable huddles. They were the last of the unmechanized agricultural work-force and if there are still those who regard their lives as an idyll, they should borrow the sugar-beet tool from where it hangs among the by-gones in the village pub and try doing a couple of rows across a field on a day such as this. It was killing. 'The wuss job on the farm!' they reckoned. The beet went by lorry to the factory at Bury St Edmund's, tumbling off all the way, which would have been a godsend with any other vegetable, but who could eat a sugar-beet except as sugar?

Someone who belonged to the first circle of my friends has died with the old year. As with other members of the original group, there has to be a gap. But I sense less a broken ring than a coming together of these early companions elsewhere. I also see, not the octogenerian, but the light figure aboard the yacht as it dips and sways its way from some Suffolk river towards the coast. I write to his wife, doing my best to keep the clichés out of the condolence. His far from deathly face looks out from the obituaries in the newspapers and is saying that there are plenty of voyages to come. And indeed there were when the photograph was taken. It reminded me suddenly of holiday snaps in Cornwall and of first circle friends climbing on Bodmin Moor.

> There were then five of us, and here are the
> Photographs to prove it, not creviced a scrap,
> And as immaculate as the words which we
> Rang round the Cheesewring, and not one of us
> A day older than we would like to look now.
> But three quick and two dust. Admire how well
> The film holds us each in shape! See, a blue day.
> Look, no shadows. Praise its brightness.

It is the Epiphany, my most mysterious feast. I come to it via music.

METAMORPHOSIS

There is more poignancy in writing nineteen-something for the last time than in writing twenty-something for the first time, or so I feel. Panic swept Christian Europe in one-thousand-and-something. The Last Judgement would arrive. But Lief Ericsson, the explorer, accidentally discovered New-foundland, a marvellous place, apparently, due to it being covered with grapes (cranberries actually) and wheat which you didn't have to sow (Lyme grass actually). He called it Wineland (Vinland, as we say). It won't be long before the young will be saying, 'Meet my grandfather. He was born in the twentieth century!'

David the retired farmworker and still hardworking bellringer and I pause to see the latest development of the barn which is being turned into a house. A huge house. David's house would go into it six times. They have stripped the barn of its rafters and it stands by the side of the main road like a naked man between roles, his old clothes in one pile, his new in another. 'They', the planners, have insisted that this building must tell everybody that it is both a barn and a house. It belonged to one of those ancient farm-manors whose deeds go back to Stephen and Matilda, or to some other millennium, heaven knows which. A tidy while ago anyway, David reckons. We can both remember when it was filled with corn and later with the kind of cars which don't go, but whose owners don't get rid of them because they own equally useless barns. Vintage car collectors roll their eyes and lick their lips when they pass a barn like ours. Youthful carpenters in hard hats and jeans swing around. They are caging these gaunt ribs and struts, each as rough as if it had just been pulled out of the hedge, in strong white rafters. Their work is swift and skilful and a treat for two idlers to watch. Through these intersections we can glimpse, for the first time in modern history, the ochre shape of the hall itself looming from its moat. It speaks. It says, 'Gone away,' and things such as, 'It happens all the time.' Meaning change. The field on the other side of the road from which the blue wagons creaked at harvest is bordered with Edwardian villas put up three years ago. Also by the Farm Shop, blessed institution. Gliders come to take a look. Thin beams, skeletal planes and myself not so fat in spite of all the seasonal eating. I leave David looking. What a bonus for village dog-walkers in January to have something like this going on. I think of my old friends who brought up their family here and who are now on Bodmin Moor among the dolmens and choughs.

Wormingford Evensong on the first Sunday of the final year. But before this, 'Now I say that the heir, as long as he is a child, differeth nothing from a servant, though he be lord of all; but is under tutors and governors, until the time appointed of the father' – the Epistle for the Sunday after Christmas. When 1999 goes out with his scythe, the next thousand years will come in as a little boy.

THE JANUARY WALKERS

The Saturday walkers pass. The Death brothers with their leaping dogs, three elderly engineers doing the round. We are fortunate as a village in possessing several round walks, that past my house being one of the best. Just before tea on Saturdays, regular as clockwork, it rumbles with brotherly talk and breaks into paroxysms of joy as the setters spy me. The solitary walker is the doctor-artist or the qualified rambler with his maps and gear. Each pauses at the isolated house, as I have halted on some remote track in Cornwall or Wales when suddenly confronted by domesticity and a figure sowing in neat rows. I am actually tackling the dead heart of things or, to be concise, the vast lifeless trunk which for a decade at least has dominated the otherwise thriving hazel in the front hedge. I will have it out at last, I told myself. I will pollard it a few feet from the ground. It will sway, topple, blackened nests, varicose ivy stems and all. And this year's catkins and nuts will appear in a new light. But although sawn through, the dead heart of things refuses to budge. It balances on its stump like some particularly challenging work of art on its pedestal. Moreover, it is immensely bigger than anyone strolling past it could have imagined. 'I'll see about this!' I told myself, fetching ropes – and vaguely recalling what I had been advised when exploring a wood in New South Wales. Which was to recognize a 'widow-maker' when you saw it – i.e., a rotten branch which you think you can pull down by yourself. And so, standing clear, I tugged the rope and rocked the heart and it slid from its plinth and stood upright among the hellebores for nearly a minute until it crashed. Who would have thought that the old pollard had so much firewood in her – and was so iron hard! It took until dark to turn it into logs. Meanwhile the walkers drifted by, extravagantly healthy and their faces lit up with Saturday delight, and brazen robins and blackbirds got under my feet, people and birds calling out.

Few in church these January days. At Mount Bures eleven of us sing

Matins (plus four hymns) without an organist, and the same morning a different eleven sing Matins (plus four hymns) at Little Horkesley with an organist. Our breath makes small plumes which float about the chapel. An Epiphany collect asks that we may both perceive and know what things we ought to do, so I preach, if that is the word, on perception. The two or three – well, ten or eleven – gathered together in Thy name stare into the chilly purity which winter ushers around old aisles and altars. Back home I read Langland on the walkers of his day, 'the tramps and beggars hastening on their rounds', the pilgrims 'full of clever talk', the 'troops of hermits' and indeed the whole of medieval England afoot. But it was May. And everyone asking what things they ought to do, no doubt.

From Ronald Blythe's current work in progress, *Out of the Valley: More Words from Wormingford*, to be published by Viking in spring 2000.

BARBARA TRAPIDO

....

Jacopo's Room

Jacopo's room is perfect. This is what he tells Hermione. She is the landlady. Prospective landlady. 'You've made it all so *perfect*.' He looks round at her rug and furniture and pictures. Then he confesses that he has his own things. He has had them shipped from Milan and they are waiting for him in a warehouse. The place where he is newly employed has paid for the shipping and the storage. 'I could get rid of them,' he says. 'It's just that they're a bit precious. They were left to me by a friend.'

Hermione glances at Jacopo, trying not to look too concerned. Jacopo is young, tall, thin, light brown and very beautiful. He has Afro hair which he wears close-cropped over a well-shaped skull. He has those eyes that come as one of the benefits of mixed-race parentage – eyes that look permanently as if they've been enhanced with black eyeliner. His eyelashes are long and black. He has a slight peachy glow on the skin across his cheek bones. Jacopo has the sort of nearly-white Afro looks that modelling agencies go mad for. He has a sweet smile and slightly girlish gestures. Hermione wonders whether the 'friend' was a partner who died of Aids. Or was she an older woman who loved him and remembered him in her will? She can tell that older women will all love Jacopo. She has only just met him and already she longs to be his mother.

'It's no problem,' she says, knowing that it will be, because Herman will go bonkers if she stashes her stuff in the garage and the shed can't possibly accommodate it all. Perhaps she can disperse it between the sheds and store rooms of her several friends? They will all, of course, love Jacopo as she does. Recklessly, she co-opts their goodwill in the cause of Jacopo's things.

'It's such a pity,' Jacopo says, now that he's got his own way. 'It's all so *perfect* as it is. You've made it all so perfect.'

Jacopo loves his room. It's not so much a room as a one-roomed cottage. It stands on its own at the end of the garden, obscured from the main house by a hedge of tall bamboo. It has bougainvillaea rampant over its brick-tiled roof and a nice little paved terrace with a small round table that reminds him of pavement cafés and two aluminium chairs. Azaleas grow on the terrace and, along one side, there's a passion-fruit vine with fruits like purple hen's eggs. The room has an *en suite* shower and loo and there's a kitchen alcove with a doll-sized fridge and a new Baby Belling and a row of stainless steel pots. Once he has his things, Jacopo knows he will be able to play house here. He loves the idea of playing house. He has never before not shared.

On his first afternoon in the room he bakes biscuits in the tiny oven – four chocolate-chip cookies on a baking sheet eight inches square – and he eats them out on his terrace, sitting on one of the aluminium chairs. An avocado tree and two palm trees with papayas are visible over his roof. He thinks that, after his various student digs in London and Bristol, and then his year on the Piazza Aspromonte, being here is like living in the country. Yet he's five minutes' walk from the drama department where he works. He's astonished by the lushness of his home town, which he can barely remember, since he left it at sixteen.

Jacopo's room is perfect. It is perfectly monochrome. He has rolled up Hermione's Kurdish rug and has added it to the pile of her furniture she's made in the shed. The walls are white and the curtains are undyed linen. The floor has those black bricks that come scored with diamond patterns. Each morning he covers his divan bed with a thick, white linen spread and on it he places his three nearly-white feather cushions. These are big and square and covered in ivory wool. Ivory and graphite. The cushion fronts are quartered in four ten-inch squares. The top right-hand square and the bottom left are cross-hatched as if with a 6B graphite pencil. The top left and the bottom right are plain.

Alongside his bed Jacopo has a neat little fifties desk with lots of miniature drawers and a pull-out writing surface on which he keeps a pad of Fabriano drawing paper and a jar of drawing pencils. He has two chrome anglepoise lamps on stepped Art Deco bases. One is on the desk and the other is beside his bed. He has a tall, glass-fronted bookcase – a barrister's bookcase – made by Globe-Wernicke and a single armchair covered in calico. His coffee table is a child's slatted wooden sledge. His three pictures are black and white. Two engravings, beautifully mounted, and one framed exhibition poster. The engravings are eighteenth century, made from sketches of Renaissance equestrian sculpture. The poster is Giacommetti. His espresso jug sits permanently on the Baby Belling. It's a nice one with a horizontal, jutting handle that makes it look like a *chocolatière* in a Chardin painting.

Twice a week, Jacopo hangs his laundry on the whirly line to the right of his terrace. All his laundry is white except for his jeans. All his bed linen is white; all his underwear, shirts and T-shirts. Hermione notices that he buys special soap powder for 'whites' because he stores it in her wash-house to which he has rights of access. He also has rights to swim in the family pool.

Jacopo has come back after ten years abroad, but Hermione does not know that. Between his name and his unplaceable accent, she assumes that he's from Europe. Perhaps he is the child of diplomats and has attended an international school in England? Perhaps his mother is an art dealer or a painter? Jacopo remembers his first bedsit in Croydon and the gas fire with broken teeth. He lived on Alpen and strawberry yoghurt for two years until he learned to cook. He did his A-levels at the college of FE. Then he went to uni. Afterwards he went to the Le Coq Mime School in Milan. Then back to England. Bristol. Thanks to Jack, he now has a Ph.D. on the *Comédie-Italienne*, but he hasn't seen Jack for quite a while. Now he's been head-hunted back home. Or is it home? Anyway, he's here. In the garden cottage.

He knows that the garden cottage which he rents will once have been a sort of kennel for black domestic servants. It will have been extended and re-roofed. Instead of the brick-tiled floor and the track-lighting and the electric points and the vitreous china WC and the paved terrace with azaleas, it will have had a single cold tap fixed to the outside wall and a concrete hole for a lavatory and a supply of cheap candles and interior walls blackened with smoke from a primus stove and a concrete floor and an orange-box for a cupboard and newspaper over one small, high window. It will have had a corrugated asbestos roof with spiders and mosquitoes coming in through the half-moon gaps. He knows these things, because his mother was a domestic servant. Maybe she still is? What he doesn't know is that, twenty-seven years earlier, his mother lived in this place. Hermione's place. It was from this place that Theodora was summarily dismissed.

In the main house, beyond the bamboo hedge, across the lawn and the swimming pool, a gold Parker pen had gone missing one morning, and Theodora's employer accused her of stealing it. He dismissed her with a week's wages and said she was lucky he wasn't calling the police. She knew that the Madam would have believed her denials, but unfortunately the Master had seen fit to throw her out while the Madam was off visiting her cousins in England. The pen had been filched by the family's eight-year-old daughter, who'd fancied using it to write her end-of-year exams.

The child thought the pen would bring her luck and so it did, because she came top of the class and never looked back. She was allowed to wear a special badge and the teacher gave her a rosette. Her name was in the school magazine. 'Daddy, I borrowed your pen,' she said and pulled it out of her schoolbag. 'Don't be cross,' she said. By that time Theodora and her cardboard suitcase and her two-week-old foetus were well on the road. It was called 'going back to the farm'. When the Madam returned she said, 'But, darlings, where's Theodora?' The children shrugged. 'She went back to the farm,' they said.

'Jacopo's Room' is an extract from Barbara Trapido's current work in progress, *Having Sex with Stravinsky* (working title), to be published by Hamish Hamilton in 2000.

MATTHEW KNEALE

....

Mesmerizing the Pig

Timothy Renshaw August–September 1857

The surprise of nearly being murdered by pirates had a quietening effect
on all aboard the *Sincerity*, myself included, and for a time even Dr Potter
and Mr Wilson treated each other with something approaching civility. It
did not last, needless to say. Once we crossed the equator our vicar began
to look restless, and it was then he started praying aloud at first light, which
he called 'dawn godliness'. That drove me halfway to distraction, as his
moaning came straight through the holes in the partition wall, while Potter
didn't look pleased at all. Soon after that there was the business of the mug
of tea that was found on the vicar's Bible, which was answered in turn by
a new and longer list of parson's laws. Even that wasn't enough for Wilson,
and in his next Sunday sermon he insisted on lecturing us about we must
look deep into our hearts and cast out all envy and wickedness, hurling,
as he spoke, little saintly smiles in the doctor's direction. When the sermon
moved next to praising the virtue of deference, and saying how it was the
God-given duty of those 'of junior station' to obey their 'natural betters',
Potter's face turned quite clenched.

It was that sermon that decided the next course of their little war. The
moment it was finished the doctor marched across to Captain Kewley,
while Wilson – who had seen his rage – followed just behind. I went too,
being curious. Their feud was the nearest thing there was aboard the *Sincerity*
to something happening, while, finding each party quite as annoying as
the other, as I did, I suppose it afforded me some faint satisfaction to watch
them assail one another.

'It occurs to me,' Potter began, 'that it might be of interest to the crew
if I delivered a few educational lectures, perhaps on scientific matters.'

Wilson cut in before Kewley had a chance to answer. 'What a generous thought, Doctor. Though I should say that such a thing would hardly be suitable for the sabbath, when we prefer to reflect upon the spiritual.'

His thinking, I supposed, was that Kewley would not want lectures cluttering up the ship's workdays, and so Potter's proposal would be squeezed nicely into oblivion. He was probably right, too. Where he made his mistake was in being so very pushing. A weary look passed across Kewley's face. 'I don't see why we shouldn't have room for his talk as well as yours, Vicar. After all, the doctor's science is also part of the Good Lord's world, is it not?'

Wilson wriggled his best but, I was pleased to see, the captain would have none of his bullying. So it was that the ship became quite a library of scribbling, as my two colleagues worked upon their discourses like swordsmen sharpening their blades, each casting his face into the most serious expression, as if to demonstrate the superiority of his work over the other's.

It was early that same week that the weather began to change. The wind had been blowing strongly until then, propelling us swiftly southwards, and already the sun had begun to lose a little of its strength, its light turning subtly whiter, reminding us that we were venturing towards a part of the world where the season was still late wintertime. On the Thursday the wind backed round from the south-west, feeling suddenly chilly, and troubling the crew with a good work with the sails. Then on the Saturday morning it dropped away to nothing and we found ourselves becalmed, and that night the fog came. By Sunday morning the vessel was encased tighter than a hand in a glove. The light was so dim and the air so still that it felt almost as if we were not at sea at all, but were inside some kind of murky room. Looking out over the side the water was visible only for a few yards, while upwards the masts and sails vanished into the whiteness.

It was around noon that we heard a loud splash off the port bow, sudden and shocking in the stillness. We all hurried to the rail, though we could see nothing but fog. Captain Kewley even called out, 'Ahoy there,' but there came no answer. Only when we stood, carefully listening, did we become aware of a sound from the same direction, faint and rhythmic, deep and low.

'It's creatures,' said Kewley in a whisper.

It seemed there were a good number of them, and as we listened their breathing grew slowly louder, until it extended all about the vessel, as if we were in the middle of some huge ocean dormitory. None of the beasts ventured close enough to be seen, and I could only presume they must be some form of whale or grampus. It may seem foolish and yet I found their invisible presence unsettling, while even the Manxmen, who I would have expected to be used to such oddities, went about their work with furtive looks, speaking in lowered voices, quite as if the huge animals were listening.

Our two Sunday lecturers, by contrast, seemed little interested, being both far more concerned with the discourses they were to give, leafing hurriedly through their notes, or disagreeing with one another over the construction of the temporary pulpit. Dr Potter was to speak first. He forwent Wilson's dramatic preamble, simply marching on to the platform, from where he peered down at us with a serious look. 'My lecture today concerns the process of animal magnetism, that is also known as mesmerism,' he declared solemnly, pausing for a moment as one of the creatures produced a faint blowing sound, eerie through the fog, 'and will be concluded with a practical demonstration of this most important process, in which I hope to reveal great secrets of the soul of man.'

His intention was, I supposed, to outshine Wilson's sermonizing, and perhaps to deliver a few stabs along the way. To this end his choice seemed clever enough, mesmerism being a phenomenon of great popularity, which had filled more than a few music halls with eager watchers, delighted by the spectacle of some poor fool believing himself a donkey or bereft of a leg. I was quite intrigued myself, in fact, having never guessed the doctor was a practitioner of such an art. Rather to my surprise, however, the Manxmen seemed little pleased. For a moment I assumed they were still troubled by the presence of the sea creatures, but no, from their looks they seemed to be regarding the doctor with real dislike. I could only imagine they feared some form of joke might be played upon them. Wilson, who was sitting on a coil of rope well away from the proceedings – having insisted that 'sadly' he could not listen as he must attend to his sermon – had also observed the crew's displeasure, and was visibly smirking.

Potter himself pressed on regardless. The first part of his discourse dealt with something he termed 'the geography of the mind'. It was a subject I knew little about, and I found it interesting enough in its way. He asserted that the brain was divided into many segments, almost in the manner of an orange, each of which contained one 'impulse', many of these being a moral quality. These varied no less than human character itself, extending from wisdom to a fondness for sweet food, and from anger to a fear of heights. The power of each impetus would alter from one man to the next, and their strength or weakness would, when combined together, define the moral character of each individual. Thus a man with pronounced impulses of bravery and loyalty would make an excellent soldier, while another, who was weak in honesty and strong in greed, would likely fall into thieving. Between different races of men, as the doctor told us, variety was far greater still, as the very structure of the brain would alter. Thus we learned that the Chinese possessed a unique impulse of delight in bright colours, while among savages of Africa there was a complete absence of the impulse of civilization.

'It is mesmerism that can unlock these wonders of the mind,' Potter explained. 'Each impulse of the brain extends to the skull, and so, once a man is brought into the correct state of entrancement, the different elements of his brain can be made to reveal themselves simply by touches of the operator's fingers, in a fashion remarkable to behold. It is, indeed, quite as if one is playing upon the keys of an organ. Press upon the segment of fear and the subject will at once show signs of great alarm, perhaps believing that a fearful chasm has opened up in front of him. Try deceitfulness and his every utterance will be untrue. Touch confession and he will admit to all manner of secrets. Ten minutes of mesmerism can reveal a man far more truthfully than months studying his apparent nature.'

Some of the crewmen, I noticed, were showing signs of restlessness, tapping their feet upon the deck.

'Mesmerism pays no heed to titles or other grand frippery. Enchant a pauper and you may discover him to be wiser than a lord,' Potter continued, undeterred. He cast a sudden glance towards the vicar, 'and a simple butcher's boy may be found richer in virtue than a priest.'

So there was his first stab. Wilson's smirk vanished and he buried himself in his notes.

Pleased with this little piece of violence, Potter stepped to the front of the temporary pulpit and peered down through the fog. 'This, I hope, will have made clear the theory behind this most important process. The moment has now come to offer a practical demonstration, so you may see for yourselves, and for this I must ask for the assistance of a volunteer.'

I had expected that this might prove awkward and I was not wrong. Potter smiled, and waited, only to find himself answered with a wall of silence. Soon the creaking timbers and water lapping against the ship's side seemed loud indeed. The doctor looked quite taken aback.

'Surely there is somebody?' Just as he was beginning to look a touch alarmed, the chief mate raised his hand. Potter broke into a smile. 'Thank you, Mr Brew.'

'Ah, but I'm not offering,' Brew declared, grinning in a way that looked hardly reassuring. 'I'm just asking what'll happen to the lucky body that does. Will you have him strip himself naked thinking he's a bunny rabbit?'

The crew let go a faint ripple of snickering.

Potter looked troubled. The very last thing he wanted was for his lecture to be turned into some kind of joke. He attempted to retrieve the mood of seriousness as best he could, assuring us all, with an awkward smile, 'I have not the slightest interest in theatrical games. The fact is that mesmerism, besides being an invaluable tool of science, is also a most natural state in which to enter, being wonderfully calming to the nerves. While some persons are more susceptible than others, I do believe that there is hardly a single man or woman who cannot safely be brought into such a condition.'

The Manxmen did not laugh at this little speech, it was true, but none of them volunteered either. So it was that the doctor made the mistake of trying to reassure us further. 'It is, indeed, a process quite as normal and healthy as sleep. Why, there are numerous recorded instances even of animals becoming mesmerized, while in some cases that I . . .'

He got no further. Up went Brew's hand like a semaphore arm. 'Animals, did you say?' He tilted his head to one side, all dangerous innocence. 'Well, there's a thing, is there not? I wonder, Doctor, could you mesmerize one of the swineys for us then? You know, just so we can see how it's done.'

This brought more than just looks and snickering. Mylchreest the steward uttered a curious squeaking giggle and this was enough to unleash all the rest. I will admit I laughed myself, while Wilson turned about on his coil of rope, clearly delighting in the spectacle. As for Potter, he was beginning to look greatly disconcerted. He had intended this occasion to be one when he would revenge himself on his enemy, and instead found himself humiliated before the whole ship, caught in that purgatory between feigned seriousness and open ridicule. It was quite a sight, especially in one who, until now, I had never seen lose command of himself.

'I'm not sure that would be useful,' he declared, with the stiffest of smiles.

He would have been wiser just to say a very plain no. As it was, Brew pretended to take his words as some form of encouragement, nodding his head as if in agreement. 'Wouldn't we all love to see it, though, Doctor?' He glanced about him, stirring the rest into agreement.

'But I have no experience of any such thing,' Potter declared weakly.

'Ah, you're doing yourself down,' said Brew, now maliciously supportive. 'A clever fellow like you would manage it easier than kicking.'

I believe the doctor would have wriggled his way free even then had it not been for Captain Kewley. Until this moment he had kept aloof from the whole matter, but now he gave the surgeon a sly look. 'Come along, Doctor,' he called out in a cheerful voice. 'We're far too interested to be put off now. Mesmerize a swiney for us, there's a good fellow.'

Potter threw the captain a desperate glance, I suppose hoping he might show pity and make a joke of his suggestion, but it was in vain. The rest of the crew were already urging him on with shouts and cheers, and so, with as much enthusiasm as a condemned man strolling to his gibbet, he began making his way forward through the fog. Wilson left his coil of rope to follow, as did I. Reaching to the boat that served as the pigsty, the doctor looked quite crushed. Why, I would have felt quite sorry for him if I had not had to suffer his company through all those long weeks.

The reason that a pig had been proposed rather than any other creature was simple enough. We had eaten almost all the rest. All the bullocks were gone, and the chickens too, while of the sheep only one sorry specimen survived. Pigs were usually kept till last, being regarded as the best sailors, and three of the four of the animals still remained, all berthed in the main boat. As Potter and his audience gathered around this, the poor beasts showed some alarm, cowering and snorting, which was hardly surprising seeing as they had witnessed so many of their fellow animals being taken, one by one, to the rear of the vessel and noisily dispatched from this world.

'Don't you go crowding them,' the cook, Quayle, protested, seeming the only one displeased by the turn of events. 'I won't have them upset.'

Of the three beasts, two were sows while the third was a male, huge and sagging, with the most disquieting eyes: mournfully alert, as if he understood only too plainly the temporary nature of his situation. Potter stroked his beard, seeming now resigned to attempting the task forced upon him.

'The method I will use,' he announced cautiously, 'is the same as I have employed upon men, though there is no certainty that it will prove as effective on animals.'

It was the male he picked, I suppose because this seemed the most human-like of the three. He reached out towards the creature, looking it firmly in the eye, and then began passing his hands about its head in a kind of stroking movement, though without ever quite touching its skin. Whether this was part of his technique, or simple avoidance of the mud and worse with which the animal was caked, was hard to know. As for the pig itself, it flinched away at first, but then gradually seemed to grow calmer, and after a time appeared even to be quite enjoying the process, meeting the doctor's mesmerizing stare with a dozy look of its own. Gradually the movements of Potter's hands extended, until they reached halfway down the creature's back and he was leaning right into the boat. Then, peering determinedly at the beast, he drew back.

'The animal,' he announced, suddenly proud, 'is now entranced.'

This won a hush of respect, and surprise too. Before the doctor could proceed any further, though, the creature uttered a loud snort and began sniffing among the pieces of muck and old food at the bottom of the boat. Potter ignored the sniggers that followed, looking now serious. It seemed the exercise had now caught his curiosity, causing him to forget his earlier reluctance. 'There is another method that I can try which may prove more suitable to animals,' he declared. 'This involves the subject intently staring at an object until entranced.'

My curiosity was how the pig would know that he was supposed to stare at anything. In the event I never discovered. Potter's mistake, as I see it now, was that he did not arrange matters before he started. He was too impatient to place the creature once again into a receptive state – which he did with the same stroking and staring as before – and it was only when the animal began to respond, looking dozy, that he troubled himself with what mesmerizing object he would use.

'What I now need,' he said in a soft voice, never turning from the pig's small, doleful eyes, 'is something bright and reflective. Anything of polished metal will do.'

For a moment the Manxmen looked at one another, uncertain. Then the chief mate, Brew, reached to his waistband. It is possible, of course, that his choice was just accident, but considering the man's character this seemed unlikely. He passed the object into the outstretched hand and then, as Potter brought this before him, both he and the pig found themselves looking at a long, shining knife.

The doctor saw the danger at once, pulling the blade back to hide it from the animal's sight, but it was too late. I had no idea that a pig could make so great a noise. All at once the air became filled by a hideous squealing: a sound of pure, rawest fear. At the same instant he began plunging irresistibly about the longboat, quite like some steam locomotive, with the sows following just behind, their pen rocking violently from side to side, hay spilling into the air like coal dust, and the metal tubs that held their food banging and crashing as they were hurled back and forth. The Manxmen did their best to retrieve the situation, leaning forward with outstretched arms, but the fact is that three pigs in full flight are not easily stopped, especially when they are slippery with mud and dung. The wiser policy might well have been simply to leave the poor creatures be, as every grabbing hand encouraged their panic. Finally, though, the sows were halted, and then China Clucas, the ship's giant, managed to catch the main beast by its tail, and though all three screeched dreadfully, the scene in the pen began to show signs of greater calm.

As to what followed, even now I could not say if it bore any connection with what had just occurred, or if it was merely a coincidence of timing. It seemed to follow, certainly, but the mind will sometimes play tricks at such a moment of excitement, seeing unconnected events as so many links in a chain. In truth I could not even say if sea creatures possess the power

'Mesmerizing the Pig' is an extract from Matthew Kneale's current work in progress, *English Passengers*, to be published by Hamish Hamilton in March 2000.

of hearing, let alone if they concern themselves with sounds emerging from beyond their watery domain. The fact remained, however, that hardly had the pigs been stilled when there was a momentous watery crash from somewhere beyond the port bow. We never saw what ocean acrobatics the beast had got up to, on account of the fog, but the consequence was clear as could be. The ship, which had been still as land, began suddenly and violently rolling.

For a moment I thought we had suffered nothing worse than surprise. A ship, after all, is well used to a bit of tipping. Then, though, I became aware of the excited chattering in Manx on the further side of the boat, and realized they were all looking at Clucas's arm, which he was holding with his hand in a curious way, and I saw blood was spilling out between his fingers. The pig he had caught had toppled clean against him when the ship rolled, and he must have caught his wrist against a jagged corner of the creatures' water tub. Clucas himself looked pale as a ghost.

It is curious how swiftly a mood can alter. One moment we were engaged upon what was, if truth be told, an unkind joke. Half an instant later all were grave faces. The greatest change, though, came to Potter. All at once he was transformed from dupe to hero.

'Have my case brought,' he commanded. So he set to work.

The sea creatures did not stay long after that, and the fog was gone by the next morning. As for Clucas, within just a day or two he was recovered enough to sit quietly on deck in the cool sunshine, offering respectful greetings to his saviour whenever he came near. It was perhaps hardly a surprise that, from that afternoon, nobody, including Brew, tried to make a joke of the doctor. Potter even treated us to another lecture the next Sunday – this one on the benefits of vegetarianism – and, much to Wilson's annoyance, his audience stood through the whole thing quiet as lambs.

ROGER McGOUGH

....

A Serious Poem

This is a serious poem
It wears a serious face
It will not fritter away the words
It knows its place.

Perfectly balanced
Neither too long nor too short
It gazes solemnly heavenwards
Like a real poem ought.

Familiar with the classics
It drops names with ease.
Here comes Plato with Lycidas
And look, there's Demosthenes!

A serious poem will often end
With two lines that rhyme.
But not always.

Roger McGough's new collection of poetry, *The Way Things Are*, is published by Viking.

FERGAL KEANE

....

Christmas in Cape Town

We came home in darkness and cold. Lost to us the big skies, the warmth and sunshine. Home to little streets, terraced houses and the silence of Christmas roads. How forbidding and sad London looks in the early dark, a city trudging cold and tired into the last days of the year. At such moments I wonder why I am living here. And I come up with just one answer: work. Just the work. What a grim admission.

Sorry, Londoners, I try to like the city of my birth but it really is a struggle, especially after Christmas in Cape Town. The taxi-driver tried his best to console us on the way in from Heathrow. He said the weather was mild compared to last week. Nine degrees and holding. But what did he know? The day before as we flew out of Cape Town it was hovering around thirty with the sun glancing on the blue water at Camps Bay and the beach crowded with the children of the southern summer.

Paragliders sailed over the rim of Table Mountain, their shadows like the wings of giant hawks swooping down the mountain towards the green suburbs. Out on the bay, ferries were plying tourists back and forth to Robben Island on a calm sea. The political prison where Nelson Mandela spent most of his twenty-seven years in jail has become a tourist mecca. When I first came to the city in the early eighties, Mandela was still in residence and tourists, or any kind of visitors, would have been arrested for approaching the island. How things change.

Having spent several weeks working in the dust and squalor of the squatter camps around Johannesburg, I was ready for Cape Town. I know that the city's critics deride it as an island of privilege in a country weighed down by the legacy of apartheid.

Driving in from the airport the traveller cannot fail to notice the vast squatter encampments which are separated from the city by the imposing bulk of Table Mountain. And, yes, some of the local whites are unbearably smug about their good life between the mountain and sea. Worse still are the new European arrivals who have bought vast houses and established themselves as a kind of imported gentry. 'Eurotrash', the locals contemptuously call them.

But none of my reservations can take anything away from the seductive beauty of the Cape. It is the landscape that draws me back time and again; landscape and, of course, the friendships forged in the darker days of the South African story. A Canadian friend who had gone to Kenya for Christmas gave us the use of his home on the slopes overlooking Camps Bay. Most days we took to the road, exploring the beaches and coves of the Cape coast: Noordhoek, with its great expanse of white sand and blue water; Scarborough and Witsands, where the light sea mist drapes the rocks and dunes in late afternoon; and Hout Bay, where we spent Christmas Day.

It rained in the morning and Father Thornton's plans for an open-air mass were hastily abandoned. And so we crowded into the tiny church, to listen to the elderly priest's pious exaltations and breathe in the smoke of incense which his helpers liberally swept along the aisles. Being not remotely pious and an individual of some imperfection, I always feel guilty when I go to mass. It is a sense that everybody around me is 'good' and that I am not. I am also an infrequent observer of Catholic ritual. My friend Father Dick, an Irish priest whom we met for Christmas lunch, said it didn't matter as long as you made the effort. But I am pursued by Catholic guilt and it took several bottles of good South African wine to rescue me from my sombre meditations.

I am happy to report that for the first time in my life I ate Christmas lunch at a restaurant. And also for the first time I did not eat turkey and ham. Such bravery at the age of thirty-seven! The small Indian restaurant on the beach was serving baked lamb and baby chicken. It was a long and happy lunch, one of the best Christmas Days I can remember.

There was only one depressing moment. An elderly German arrived at the restaurant accompanied by a large white dog. The man was old enough to have had an interesting past and his political opinions suggested a strong right-wing inclination. He told us the dog was a cross between a wolf and a husky. And then a black beggar approached. The dog growled menacingly. The German barely restrained the beast and shrugged the beggar away. 'If you want money, go and ask Mandela for it,' he barked.

It is the standard reply of the disgruntled white who cannot bear the reality of a black-ruled South Africa. Blacks knocking on white doors looking for jobs hear it all the time. It suggests, at the very least, a remarkable absence of humility on the part of the former ruling class. What do they think South Africa would have been like without Mandela and his gift of reconciliation and forgiveness? After several glasses of wine my capacity for indignation was ripe. I was about to read the riot act to our German friend when Father Dick pulled me back. 'It is Christmas Day, let it go,' he said.

He was right. Christmas Day is not a time for arguments. And so we climbed into Dick's car and headed for Cape Point in search of baboons. I had told my nearly-three-year-old that the Cape was full of monkeys and apes. The prospect of a meeting thrilled him greatly. But so far they had been noticeably reluctant about showing themselves. 'Where are the baboons, Dad?' came the insistent question every evening as we drove home after another apeless day.

Just outside Simonstown on a narrow stretch of road between mountain and sea we encountered a large family group. They sat in the road and stopped the traffic. The bolder ones climbed on to cars and began to beg for food. A bus full of Chinese tourists stopped directly ahead of us. Hands appeared out of the windows, one of them trying to stroke the head of a male baboon. We honked our horn furiously. A baboon's bite is particularly ferocious and they are, however familiar with humans, still wild animals. The Chinese were puzzled by our concern. It reminded me of an incident when I was living in South Africa in the early nineties and a group of Chinese visited a lion park outside Johannesburg. Two of the group got out of their vehicle and posed for a picture with the lions. The result: two dead Chinese tourists. But my son was delighted by the spectacle on the road ahead of us. Baboons on Christmas Day! Will he remember it when he grows up? I'd like to think he would but I suppose not. I will, though.

On the night before leaving for home we travelled out to the winelands for a barbecue on the farm of my friends, Richard and Silvanna. Richard is a cameraman whom I came to know while living in South Africa. We still work together from time to time. But these days most of his efforts are taken up with fruit farming. It is as far away as you can imagine from battlefields and squatter camps. A saner life.

His farm sits below the Great Drakenstein mountain near the town of Franschoek. There are rows of peach and nectarine and apple trees. There are horses and some ducks and even some baboons and wild boar who raid the fruit orchards at night. As dusk came on, Richard lit the firewood and the great mountain above us melted into shadow. His four young boys disappeared into the fruit groves with our son. And we adults relaxed and opened some wine and spoke of old times on the road. It was Christmas all right but not like I'd ever known it.

Letters Home by Fergal Keane is published by Penguin.

ESTHER FREUD

....

It's William's Birthday

Jake was the only one who couldn't see the point of getting up. He yawned luxuriously and snuggled close into the gaping poster jaws of a huge grizzly bear. It was the morning of William's birthday and Tess was sitting up in bed, feverishly knitting the last diminishing rows. This second sock was very slightly shorter than the first and occasionally she stopped and gave it a quick tug. Eventually the stitches of the toe were down to six, four, two and then with one final loop the sock was closed and tightened with a knot. She bit the wool off bluntly with her teeth.

'Mum.' She raced to find the Sellotape, and there on the stairs were Doon and Sandy singing 'Happy Birthday' while Honour serenaded William on her violin.

'He's coming downstairs!' Tess screamed, and she rushed off to take her place as his daughters all began to hip-hip-hooray him into his seat.

Francine had arranged holly in a spiky crown around his bowl, and she'd made a special breakfast, muesli with apples finely grated in a curl over the top. There were small handfuls of oatmeal, barley, raisins and wheatgerm sprinkled with nuts.

'Well, thank you.' William slid on to his chair, and Tess saw his eyes counting up the cards. She wriggled with anticipation. There was no doubt her present had to be the best. William reached out and pulled the first bright package towards him and the whole table held their breath.

'Morning,' Jake said, stumbling through the door, and he took his seat as if it were just any old morning of the year. 'What's this?' He flicked at the apple, already browning on his plate, and Francine said, 'Shhh!'

'Now, I wonder who this could be from.' William beamed, holding up a lumpen round of scratchy wrapping, and Sandy put her hand over her mouth and began to squeak. 'It feels very precious,' he said, weighing it solemnly in his hand and carefully stripping back the paper to reveal a bird's nest, all old and mouldy from the ground.

'Sandy.' He leant sideways and kissed her high forehead where one chickenpox had left a small scar crescent like the moon.

'Thank you.' Tess could see he was genuinely touched.

'I found it on my own.'

'Did you now?' He reached for the next present. It was wrapped neatly, squarely, a rectangle, four corners sharp. 'I wonder what this could be?' Everybody laughed. 'It's from Francine,' he mused, turning it over as if he couldn't possibly imagine what it might be.

'It's a book,' Tess yelled. It was out before she could stop herself, and everybody's laughter died away. 'I mean . . . it might not be . . .'

William frowned over the wrapping. 'The poetry of Robert Burns.' He gave Francine an understanding smile. 'Thank you, I shall enjoy owning this again.' He touched it for a moment to his heart.

Honour had embroidered him a picture. It was old-fashioned, like a sampler, with cross-stitch at the edge and in the middle a tiny outline of a house. Beside the house a man stood with three children linked to each other at the palm, growing very slightly smaller like ducks along a pond.

'The proportions aren't quite right.' Honour craned to see, and she showed him how the man had come out bigger than the house.

'It's absolutely perfect,' he told her. 'A work of art.' He laid it across his plate with great appreciation.

'So now, what do we have here?' The roll of the next present flopped across his hand. 'It feels like a tie,' he laughed, 'or a pair of socks.' He chuckled as if it was the least likely thing in the world that it could be. Tess gulped, shivery with waiting, and saw the small worms of the apple darkening brown. And then there they were, her socks unfurling out of the paper, still warm from knitting, a mound of lumpy wool. William held one by the toe. 'They look . . . very practical.' She wanted to tell him, in case he hadn't noticed, that she'd knitted every stitch of them herself.

'Thank you. Right.' He was moving on, glancing at his watch. A bookmark from Doon and a small World Wildlife diary from Jake.

'Jake, what can I say?' William looked ridiculously pleased. 'That's wonderful,' and he let his fingers trail through the diary, stroking each page as if Jake had pledged him the whole of the next year.

'Now eat up, everyone,' he said, 'or we'll all be late for school.'

Tess tried one last time. 'Do you think you'll ever wear the socks?'

William paused, his mouth full, as if he might not recall what socks she meant. 'Oh, yes,' he nodded, chewing. 'Yes, I'm sure I'll find some opportunity for wearing them, maybe on that trip up Everest I've planned.' And he looked around the table to raise the volume of everybody's laugh.

'It's William's Birthday' is an extract from Esther Freud's current work in progress, *The Wild*, to be published by Hamish Hamilton in summer 2000.

JAMIE OLIVER

·················

My Perfect Christmas Pressie

CHRISTMAS HEADACHES

For the last five years in London Christmas has seemed to come round quicker and quicker. The build-up to Christmas in the kitchen at work has always been extremely fierce, with double shifts, double sittings, double headaches. Unfortunately, no double pay. Come the 15th of December, Peter Andre, or some other cheesy geezer, has already switched the Regent Street lights on and I have fifteen people to buy for and nothing bought. Great! So the pressure's on to buy personalized presents that will actually be used and not tossed into the back of a cupboard come New Year. Annoyingly for me, I've always been obsessed with choosing the right presents for people – it's great to see friends or family using pressies that I gave them a year or two before. Pressies don't have to be expensive, they just have to be clever – have a little bit of personality, just like cooking! Personally, I'm mad about functional pressies, things that do stuff.

So anyway, last year, what with work in the restaurant, finishing my cookbook and filming *The Naked Chef*, I felt slightly knackered, short of both time and inspiration for clever pressies. Then, looking through the first chapter of my book, 'First Move', which is all about 'wanting to make a difference to cooking at home' and having the right ingredients to hand, I became inspired and decided to put my words into action.

A PUKKA PACKAGE

What I wanted to do was give a pressie that was fully functional. The idea was to fill a box or some other container with funky jars of herbs and spices, a big jar of vanilla sugar and one of Maldon sea salt, some flavoured oils, vinegars, homemade jam and pickles and a pestle and mortar. Pukka – my mum was gonna love it! Just like in my book, you can come home with a bit of meat and fish and do anything with it, using the contents of the hamper. The good thing about this pressie is that everything is non-perishable and can be bought really cheaply; the bad thing is, you want to keep it for yourself!

CHEAP AS CHIPS!

First of all I scanned reject and seconds shops for a funky box or hamper to hold all the lovely goodies. I found a cheap one and thought it could be used afterwards for picnics or storing CDs. Lovely. In the same shop I found medium to large glass bottles and airtight jars. They had to be plain, though – some of them were disgusting with luminous patterns all over them labelled *Salt* and *Pepper*. Nah, tacky tacky! So I thought I'd go minimalist: plain and simple. They looked classy and were as cheap as chips – and that doesn't happen very often! Not back in Essex anyway.

Next stop I picked up a load of spices from a little spice shop. Best bet is to go to a true ethnic one, not your fashionable designer version. This way you know you'll get the freshest and cheapest spices as the stock is turned over regularly. I chose the basics: dried chillies, coriander, cumin, caraway and fennel seeds, dried oregano, black peppercorns, nutmeg, cloves and four fresh vanilla pods. As soon as I got home I jarred up all these spices in the medium-sized jars, putting the vanilla pods to one side (for making vanilla sugar). I filled the larger jars with Maldon sea salt and another with vanilla sugar – they looked fantastic and will keep for ages stored like this.

....

Vanilla sugar recipe
1kg/2lb caster sugar
4 vanilla pods

You need a food processor for this. Put your vanilla pods in the mixer, blitz, scrape the sides and blitz again. Add all the sugar and blitz for about 2 minutes. Sieve the mixture into a bowl, return any lumps to the food processor and blitz again. You may need to repeat this process if you want it really fine. The result will be a slightly ashy-coloured mixture – now that's real vanilla sugar!

I then needed to buy some half-decent extra virgin olive oil. I bought a four-litre canister from an Italian deli and I suggest you try to do the same. It works out much cheaper this way. I tasted three or four different varieties and went with the one I liked the best. To flavour oil is very very simple.

It's not about pretty sprigs of rosemary in a pretty bottle – leave that to M&S! What you do is take some rosemary, basil or thyme, whole lemons, dried chillies or any spices that take your fancy, and smash them up in a bowl with a rolling-pin or scrunch and bruise them with your bare hands. Pour as much oil as you need to fill one of your glass bottles into the bowl and stir, mix and scrunch so the flavours and fragrances are dispersed into it . . . tasty, tasty, tasty oil, that's what you want – not pretty, just tasty! Leave it to sit for an hour before sieving through a funnel into one of your glass bottles. Lovely; easy; done. I love using my rosemary oil on roast potatoes. Lemon oil is good massaged on to chicken before grilling, roasting or frying for a really clean and complementary flavour. Chilli oil is great over any pasta, pizzas and bread and basil oil can be used on any salad.

For the vinegars, we can be in keeping with the M&S style, as this does actually work on a more subtle level! Buy enough white wine vinegar to fill your remaining glass bottles. Put a couple of good handfuls of anything you like really – tarragon and raspberry are both pretty classic flavours – into the bottles. Personally I like a good mixed-herb vinegar (parsley, thyme, bay, basil, tarragon, marjoram) or spiced vinegar (chillies, chillies and more chillies). Once you've done that, just pour the vinegar in, close the lid and give the bottle a good shake. A dribble of spiced vinegar is great in any tomato sauce to give a piquant tang. Herb vinegar is fantastic in salsas, chutneys or salad dressings.

So the bottles are full with lovely flavoured oils and vinegars. A good idea now is to handwrite some sticky labels for each bottle suggesting the above uses. If, like me, you have the handwriting of a five-year-old, then ask a friend with reasonably legible writing to help you out!

Now, as far as jam and pickles go, I had made strawberry jam and pickled spring onions in the summer – both great ideas for a hamper – so I used those. Here are two open recipes which can jam and pickle anything, although personally I prefer to pickle chillies. I must admit I did want to add a couple of extra preserves to the hamper, so I bought some nice ones from my local market, soaked off the labels, wrote my own stickers, cut out a couple of doilies of material and used rubber bands to secure them over the lids. Yes, they looked great, yes, they tasted great, and yes, I did cheat – and I also lied and said I'd made them! You too can do this in the spirit of Christmas!!

....

Strawberry or Raspberry Jam

The only ingredients you need for making jam are fruit and sugar. Wash and hull the fruit you have chosen, then weigh it. You will need the same amount of sugar as fruit. I always use 'jam sugar' for guaranteed success as it contains pectin, a natural setting agent.

Put the fruit in a nice, big pan and simmer it over a medium heat. Stir constantly to stop it catching on the bottom of the pan. Once the fruit starts to make its own juice, you can just let it simmer gently until it is soft. Some people like whole fruit in their jam, but if you prefer you can give it a bit of a mash at this point.

Add all the sugar and stir until it has dissolved, then turn the heat right up and boil it. After it has been boiling fast for a few minutes, take about half a teaspoon of the mixture and put it on a cold saucer. Let it cool. Then push it gently with your finger and if it goes 'wrinkly', then it's done. If it doesn't, leave it to boil for another minute or two and then test it again. When the jam mixture is done, remove it from the heat. Leave it for about twenty minutes and then spoon it into your clean, warm jars and screw the lids on tight. You can make material doilies like I did and secure them over the lids with rubber bands. Lovely!

....

Pickled Chillies or Onions

200g/7oz medium green chillies or spring/pickling onions
6 black peppercorns
1 bay leaf
1 teaspoon salt
200ml/7fl oz white wine vinegar or rice vinegar
2 tablespoons caster sugar

If you're using chillies, then buy perfect green ones without blemishes (you can use red chillies but they will be slightly hotter). Carefully score from the stalk end to the tip on one side only and remove the seeds (use a teaspoon for this). Pour boiling water over the chillies, let them sit for five minutes, then drain. If using spring or pickled onions then simply peel them.

Next, put your chillies or onions, black peppercorns, bay leaf and salt into one of your airtight glass jars. Put the sugar and the vinegar into a pan and heat until the sugar is fully dissolved. When the vinegar mixture is quite hot but not boiling, pour it into the jar with the chillies or onions. Allow it to cool down before putting the lid on. Pickled like this, chillies or onions will keep in the fridge for at least three months.

Last but not least, the gem of any kitchen has to be the pestle and mortar – the oldest kitchen gadget in the world and one that can never be replaced with an electrical counterpart. For marinades, rubs, sauces or salsas, you can't beat it for bashing and bruising the flavour out of things. You can buy fantastic rock ones, which will never ever break (if you drop one on your foot it will break it, so be careful!), in Chinese or Japanese supermarkets, which are found all over the country. Failing that, you can pick up a porcelain one from most department stores – but be warned, these can crack.

PERFECT PRESSIE

Well, that's it. You've got all your lovely goodies and your empty hamper in front of you. Be as indulgent as you want when it comes to money and how much you want to spend on it. When you've done it all up, it will look as if you've spent a fortune anyway! Now get creative – arrange everything as carefully as you like or throw it all in the hamper (personally I go for the rough and rustic look) and get ready to make someone's Christmas!

The Naked Chef by Jamie Oliver is published by Michael Joseph.

ALAIN DE BOTTON

··················

A Contemporary Love Story
with Schopenhauerian Notes

A man is attempting to work on a train between Edinburgh and London. It is early in the afternoon on a warm spring day. Papers and a diary are on the table before him, and a book is open on the armrest. But the man has been unable to hold a coherent thought since Newcastle, when a woman entered the carriage and seated herself across the aisle. After looking impassively out of the window for a few moments, she turned her attention to a pile of magazines. She has been reading Vogue *since Darlington. She reminds the man of a portrait by Christen Købke of Mrs Høegh-Guldberg (though he cannot recall either of these names), which he saw, and felt strangely moved and saddened by, in a museum in Denmark a few years before. But unlike Mrs Høegh-Guldberg, she has short brown hair and wears jeans, a pair of trainers and a canary-yellow V-neck sweater over a T-shirt. He notices an incongruously large digital sports watch on her pale, freckle-dotted wrist. He imagines running his hand through her chestnut strands, caressing the back of her neck, sliding his hand inside the sleeve of her pullover, watching her fall asleep beside him, her lips slightly agape. He imagines living with her in a house in south London, in a cherry-tree-lined street. He speculates that she may be a cellist or a graphic designer or a doctor specializing in genetic research. His mind turns over strategies for conversation. He considers asking her for the time, for a pencil, for directions to the bathroom, for reflections on the weather, for a look at one of her magazines. He longs for a train crash, in which their carriage would be thrown into one of the vast barley fields through which they are passing. In the chaos, he would guide her safely outside and repair with her to a nearby tent set up by the ambulance service, where they would be offered lukewarm tea and stare into each other's eyes. Years later, they would attract interest by revealing that they had met in the tragic Edinburgh Express collision. But because the train seems uninclined to derail, though he knows it to be louche and absurd, the man cannot help clearing his throat and leaning over to ask the angel if she might have a spare Biro. It feels like jumping off the side of a very high bridge.*

1. Philosophers have not traditionally been impressed. The tribulations of love have appeared too childish to warrant investigation, the subject better left to poets and hysterics. It is not for philosophers to speculate on hand-holding and scented letters.
   Schopenhauer was puzzled by the indifference:

We should be surprised that a matter that generally plays such an important part in the life of man has hitherto been almost entirely disregarded by philosophers, and lies before us as raw and untreated material.

The neglect seemed the result of a pompous denial of a side of life which violated man's rational self-image. Schopenhauer insisted on the awkward reality:

Love . . . interrupts at every hour and most serious occupations, and sometimes perplexes for a while even the greatest minds. It does not hesitate . . . to interfere with the negotiations of statesmen and the investigations of the learned. It knows how to slip its love-notes and ringlets even into ministerial portfolios and philosophical manuscripts . . . It sometimes demands the sacrifice of . . . health, sometimes of wealth, position and happiness.

2. Like the Gascon essayist born two hundred and fifty-five years before him, Schopenhauer was concerned with what made man – supposedly the most rational of all creatures – less than reasonable. There was a set of Montaigne's works in the library of his apartment.
   Schopenhauer had read of how reason could be dethroned by a fart, a big lunch or an ingrowing toe-nail, and concurred with Montaigne's view that our minds were subservient to our bodies, despite our arrogant faith that we could exert full conscious control over ourselves.

3. But Schopenhauer went further. Rather than alighting on loose examples of the dethronement of reason, he gave a name to a force within us which he felt invariably had precedence over reason, a

force powerful enough to distort all of reason's plans and judgements, and which he termed the will-to-life (*Wille zum Leben*) – defined as an inherent drive within human beings to secure their existence, to reproduce and to look after their children. The will-to-life led even committed depressives to fight for survival when they were threatened by a shipwreck or grave illness. It ensured that the most cerebral, career-minded individuals would be seduced by the sight of gurgling infants, or if they remained cold, that they were likely to conceive a child anyway, and love it fiercely on arrival. And it was the will-to-life that provoked people to ignore their work and lose their reason over comely passengers encountered on long-distance train journeys.

4. Schopenhauer might have resented the disruption of love (it isn't easy to proffer grapes to schoolgirls); he refused to conceive of it as either disproportionate or accidental. It was entirely commensurate with love's function:

Why all this noise and fuss? Why all the urgency, uproar, anguish and exertion? . . . Why should such a trifle play so important a role . . . ? It is no trifle that is here in question; on the contrary, the importance of the matter is perfectly in keeping with the earnestness and ardour of the effort. The ultimate aim of all love-affairs . . . is actually more important than all other aims in man's life; and therefore it is quite worthy of the profound seriousness with which everyone pursues it.

And what is the aim? Neither communion nor sexual release, understanding nor entertainment. The romantic dominates life because

what is decided by it is nothing less than the composition of the next generation . . . the existence and special constitution of the human race in times to come.

It is because love directs us with such force towards child-rearing, the second of the will-to-life's two great commands that Schopenhauer judged it the most inevitable and understandable of our obsessions.

5. The fact that the continuation of the species is seldom in our minds when we ask for a phone number is no objection to the theory. We

are, suggested Schopenhauer, split into conscious and unconscious selves, the unconscious governed by the will-to-life, the conscious subservient to it and unable to learn of all its plans. Rather than a sovereign entity, the conscious mind is a partially sighted servant of a dominant, child-obsessed will-to-life:

[The intellect] does not penetrate into the secret workshop of the will's decisions. It is, of course, a confidant of the will, yet a confidant that does not get to know everything.

Our intellect understands only so much as is necessary to promote repro-duction – which may mean understanding very little:

[T]he intellect remains . . . much excluded from the real resolutions and secret decisions of its own will . . .

An exclusion which explains how we may consciously feel nothing more than an intense desire to see someone again, while unconsciously driven by a force aiming at the reproduction of the next generation.

Why should such deception even be necessary? Because, for Schopen-hauer, we would not reliably assent to reproduce unless we had first lost our minds.

6. The analysis surely violates a rational self-image; at least it counters suggestions that romantic love is an avoidable escapade from more serious tasks, that it is perhaps forgivable for youngsters with too much time on their hands to swoon by moonlight and sob beneath bedclothes, but that it is unnecessary and demented for their seniors to neglect their work *because they have glimpsed a face on a train.* By conceiving of love as biologically inevitable, key to the continuation of the species, Schopenhauer's theory of the will invited us to adopt a more forgiving stance towards the eccentric behaviour to which the emotion so often makes us subject.

The man and woman are seated at a window table in a Greek restaurant in north London. A bowl of olives lies between them, but neither can think of a way to remove the stones with requisite dignity and so they are left untouched.

She had not been carrying a Biro on her, but had offered him a pencil. After a pause, she had said how much she hated long train journeys, a superfluous remark which had given him the slender encouragement he needed. She was not a cellist, nor a graphic designer, rather a lawyer specializing in corporate finance in a City firm. She was originally from Newcastle, but had been living in London for the past eight years. By the time the train pulled into Euston, he had obtained a phone number and an assent to a suggestion of dinner.

A waiter arrives to take their order. She asks for a salad and the swordfish. She has come directly from work, and is wearing a light grey suit and the same watch. They begin to talk. She explains that on weekends her favourite activity is rock-climbing. She started at school, and has since been on expeditions to France, Spain and Canada. She describes the thrill of hanging hundreds of feet above a valley floor, and of camping in the high mountains, where, in the morning, icicles have formed inside the tent. Her dinner companion feels dizzy on the second floor of apartment buildings. Her other passion is dancing, she loves the energy and sense of freedom. When she can, she stays up all night. He favours proximity to a bed by eleven-thirty. They talk of work. She has been involved in a patent case. A kettle designer from Frankfurt has alleged copyright infringement against a British company. The company is liable under section 60.1.a of the Patents Act of 1977.

He does not follow the lengthy account of a forthcoming case, but is convinced of her high intelligence and their superlative compatibility.

1. One of the most profound mysteries of love is 'Why him?' and 'Why her?' Why, of all the possible candidates, did our desire settle so strongly on this creature, why did we come to treasure them above all others when their dinner conversation was not always the most enlightening, nor their habits the most convenient? And why, despite our best intentions, were we unable to develop a sexual interest in certain others, who were perhaps objectively as attractive and might have been more commodious to live with?

2. The choosiness did not surprise Schopenhauer. We are not free to fall in love with everyone because we cannot produce healthy children with everyone. Our will-to-life drives us towards people who will raise our chances of producing beautiful and intelligent offspring, and repulses us away from those who lower these same chances. Love is

nothing but the conscious manifestation of the will-to-life's discovery of an ideal co-parent:

The moment when [two people] begin to love each other – to fancy each other, as the very apposite English expression has it – is actually to be regarded as the very first formation of a new individual.

In initial meetings, beneath the quotidian patter, the unconscious of both parties will assess whether a healthy child could one day result from intercourse:

There is something quite peculiar to be found in the deep, unconscious seriousness with which two young people of opposite sex regard each other when they meet for the first time, the searching and penetrating glance they cast at each other, the careful inspection all the features and parts of their respective persons have to undergo. This scrutiny and examination is the meditation of the genius of the species concerning the individual possible through these two.

3. And what is the will-to-life seeking through such examination? Evidence of healthy children. The will-to-life must ensure that the next generation will be psychologically and physiologically fit enough to survive in a hazardous world, and so it seeks that children be proportioned in limb (neither too short nor too tall, too fat nor thin), and stable of mind (neither too timid nor too reckless, neither too cold nor too emotional, etc.). Our parents having made errors in their own courtships, we are unlikely to be perfectly balanced ourselves. We have typically come out too tall, too masculine, too feminine, our noses are large, our chins small. If such imbalances were allowed to persist, or were aggravated, the human race would, within a short time, founder in oddity. The will-to-life therefore pushes us towards people who can, on account of their imperfections, cancel our own (a large nose and a button nose promise a perfect nose), and hence help us restore physical and psychological balance in the next generation:

Everyone endeavours to eliminate through the other individual his own weaknesses, defects and deviations from the type, lest they be perpetuated or even grow into complete abnormalities in the child which will be produced.

The theory of neutralization gave Schopenhauer confidence in predicting pathways of attraction. Short women will fall in love with tall men, but rarely tall men with tall women (their unconscious fearing the production of giants). Feminine men who don't like sport will often be drawn to boyish women who have short hair (and wear sturdy watches):

The neutralization of the two individualities . . . requires that the particular degree of his manliness shall correspond exactly to the particular degree of her womanliness, so that the one-sidedness of each exactly cancels that of the other.

4. However charming, this theory of attraction led Schopenhauer to a conclusion so bleak, it may be best if engaged readers were to leave the next few paragraphs unread in order not to have to rethink their plans, namely, that a person who is highly suitable for our child is almost never (though we cannot realize it at the time because we have been blindfolded by the will-to-life) very suitable for us.

'That convenience and passionate love should go hand in hand is the rarest stroke of good fortune,' observed Schopenhauer. The lover who saves our child from having an enormous chin or an effeminate temperament is seldom the person who will make us happy over a lifetime. The pursuit of personal happiness and the production of healthy children are two radically different projects, which love maliciously confuses us into thinking of as one for a requisite number of years. We should not be surprised by marriages between people who would never have been friends:

Love . . . casts itself on persons who, apart from the sexual relation, would be hateful, contemptible and even abhorrent to the lover. But the will of the species is so much more powerful than that of the individual that the lover shuts his eyes to all the qualities repugnant to him, overlooks everything, misjudges everything and binds himself for ever to the object of his passion. He is so completely infatuated by that delusion, which vanishes as soon as the will of the species is satisfied, and leaves behind a detested partner for life. Only from this is it possible to explain why we often see very rational, and even eminent, men tied to termagants and matrimonial fiends, and cannot conceive how they could have made such a choice . . . A man in love may even clearly recognize and bitterly feel in his bride the intolerable faults of temperament and character which promise him a life of misery, and yet not be frightened away . . . for ultimately he seeks not his interest, but that of a third person who has yet to come into existence, although he is involved in the delusion that what he seeks is his own interest.

So, one day, a boyish woman and a girlish man will approach the altar with motives neither they nor anyone (save a smattering of Schopenhauerians at the reception) will have fathomed. Only later, when the will's demands are assuaged and a robust boy is kicking a ball around a suburban garden, will the ruse be discovered. The couple will part or pass dinners in hostile silence. Schopenhauer offered us a choice:

It seems as if, in making a marriage, either the individual or the interest of the species must come off badly.

Though he left us in little doubt as to the superior capacity of the species to guarantee its interests:

The coming generation is provided for at the expense of the present.

The man pays for dinner and asks, with studied casualness, if it might be an idea to repair to his flat for a drink. She smiles and stares at the floor. Under the table, she is folding a paper napkin into ever smaller squares. 'That would be lovely, it really would,' she says. 'But you know, like, I have to get up very early to catch a flight to Frankfurt for this meeting. Five-thirty or, like, even earlier. Maybe another time, though. It would be lovely. Really, it would.' Another smile. The napkin disintegrates under pressure.

Despair is alleviated by a promise that she will call from Germany, and that they should meet again soon, perhaps on the very day of her return. But there is no call until late on the appointed day, when she rings from a booth at Frankfurt Airport. In the background are crowds and metallic voices announcing the departure of flights to the Orient. She tells him she can see huge planes out of the window and that this place is like hell.

She says that the fucking Lufthansa flight has been delayed, that she will try to get a seat on another airline, but that he shouldn't wait. There follows a pause before the worst is confirmed. Things are a little complicated in her life right now, really, she goes on, she doesn't quite know what she wants, but she knows she needs space and some time, and if it is all right with him, she will be the one to call once her head is a little clearer.

1. The philosopher might have offered unflattering explanations of why we fall in love, but there was consolation for rejection – the consolation of knowing that our pain is normal. We should not feel confused by the enormity of the upset that can ensue from only a few days of hope. It would be unreasonable if a force powerful enough to push us towards child-rearing could – if it failed in its aim – vanish without devastation. Love could not induce us to take on the burden of propagating the species without promising us the greatest happiness we could imagine. To be shocked at how deeply rejection hurts is to ignore what acceptance involves. We must never allow our suffering to be compounded by suggestions that there is something odd in suffering so deeply. There would be something amiss if we didn't.

2. What is more, we are not inherently unlovable. There is nothing wrong with us *per se*. Our characters are not repulsive, nor our faces abhorrent. The relationship collapsed because we were unfit to produce a balanced child *with one particular person*.

3. We should with time learn to forgive our rejectors. The break-up was not their choice. Their reason may have had an appreciation of our qualities, their will-to-life did not and told them so in a way that brooked no argument – by draining them of sexual interest in us.

4. We should accept that in every clumsy attempt by one person to inform another that they need more space and time, that they are reluctant to commit or are afraid of intimacy, the rejector is striving to intellectualize an essentially unconscious negative verdict formulated by the will-to-life. We should respect the edict from nature against procreation that every rejection contains, as we might respect a flash of lightning or a lava flow – an event terrible but mightier than ourselves. We should draw consolation from the thought that a lack of love

between a man and a woman is the announcement that what they might produce would only be a badly organized, unhappy being, wanting in harmony in itself.

We might have been happy with our beloved, but nature was not – a greater reason to surrender our grip on love.

From Alain de Botton's forthcoming non-fiction work, *The Consolations of Philosophy*.

BRIAN CATHCART

The Bomb Party

For a year, in some cases a year and a half, they had been on the Hill. Half a dozen had their wives with them but the remaining eleven were on their own, several thousand miles from home. On meagre civil service pay, in conditions that were often primitive and with no holidays at all, they had worked a steady six-day week alongside their American colleagues. Creating the weapon had been much more than a job; it had been a collective mission. Now it was complete and the victory had been won, they would soon begin to leave, heading back to the British cities, British universities and British homes from which they had come. First, however, they would throw a party.

The second bomb – the really clever, really difficult design – had been dropped on 9 August and the Japanese government surrendered the following day. Within a fortnight plans for the farewell event at Los Alamos were already well advanced. A note was circulated among the British team explaining that it would take place on Saturday 22 September, when it was proposed to provide 'supper, dancing and other entertainment' for their American hosts 'in celebration of recent events'. Their government, the note said, had been persuaded to provide a sum approaching $500 to ensure that the occasion was a success, on condition that the twenty-three Britons would pay their own way as hosts, to the tune of $2.50 each.

The Hill may have been an enclosed and extremely hard-working place in the wartime years, but its residents knew how to enjoy themselves. In their own little world they had seized whatever opportunities arose, and the image of bleary-eyed scientists picking their way through the mud of half-built streets in the small hours, searching for homes identified only by random numbers, was already fixed in many minds. Even as recently as VJ Day there had been a rowdy gathering at the house of one of the Americans that ended with some ordnance boys letting off boxes of high explosive in a nearby field. If the British were to throw a party to remember – and that was their intention – they would have their work cut out.

The venue would be Fuller Lodge, one of the few relics of Los Alamos's pre-war existence as a sort of outward-bound school – the Lodge had been the boys' refectory. The central hall, with its tree-trunk columns in amber wood, its lofty ceiling and its massive stone fireplace, had a Viking ruggedness that suited the original purpose better than the present one, but it was the only possible location and its capacity of 200 represented a happy compromise between generosity and frugality (the laboratory staff by now numbered in the tens of thousands). Besides, it had the only grand piano on the Hill.

The burden of the preparations fell largely upon the six British wives. Winifred Moon took charge of the guest list, soliciting sealed envelopes with suggestions and then sifting and grouping the names until she had it right. It was a judicious mix: some scientists chosen by rank and some on grounds of friendship, some admin people, some senior military men and a smattering of lowlier soldiers personally known to the British. Wives, where available, were naturally expected too. The Oppenheimers, the Fermis, the Bethes, the Seres, the Tellers and the Weisskopfs all duly received their printed invitation cards, as did Richard Feynman, George Kistiakowsky, Louis Slotin and many others. This was a community described by a US Army general as 'the largest collection of crackpots ever seen' and the intention was to have the cream of them present on the night.

For food and drink the official kitty was supplemented by ration cards and from private funds. Despite an offer of help from the Washington mission, it was found that almost everything needed was available from military supplies at Los Alamos itself, from Santa Fe, thirty-five miles away, or *in extremis* from the more distant city of Albuquerque (rarely visited in the war years). The townsfolk in Santa Fe had been so thrilled suddenly to discover that they were neighbours to a world-famous laboratory – its purpose had been revealed only after the bombs were dropped – that no trouble was too great. The Woolworth's store, for example, lent hundreds of glasses in exchange for the most nominal deposit.

The plan was to impress the guests with a dinner and an ambience that was as English and as grand as could possibly be managed in the depths of New Mexico in 1945. This entailed a certain irony since more than a third of the hosts bore names such as Frisch, Peierls and Placzek – they were refugees only recently naturalized as British subjects – and what British style they could muster would come with a strong central European accent. Klaus Fuchs was another of these, and as one of the two members of the team to own a car, his task for the party was to buy and ferry drinks. Always efficient and obliging, Fuchs was a little stretched in the run-up to the party since he was also at that time preparing material for one of his occasional meetings down in Santa Fe with his Soviet espionage contact from New York. Once that furtive business was out of the way on Wednesday the 19th, however, and the bundle of secrets was safely on its way to Moscow, he was able to play his full part.

On the Saturday, clockwork precision was called for. The Lodge was in use throughout the day and it was 7.15 p.m. before the party team had the run of the place, so all cooking had to be done in advance at home and the food transported to the Lodge, to be kept hot in the ovens while the tables were prepared. Ernest Titterton, meanwhile, busied himself with wiring the loudspeakers. Since he had been a leading member of the team that wired the bombs, he was well qualified. Michael Poole, another clever physicist, arranged the lighting, while on the terrace a bar was set up to dispense Fuchs's purchases.

At 8 p.m. all was ready and the first guests appeared. A young scientist acting as footman barked out their names before they passed down a receiving line composed of those British team members not engaged in culinary tasks. To add further pomp to the occasion, dress was formal by American wartime standards: many men had had to take their dark suits out of mothballs, while the ladies wore their best dresses with, in a few much-admired cases, long white gloves. Robert Oppenheimer and Enrico Fermi, alas, could not attend – they were away that weekend – but the occasion still ranked as a remarkable gathering of international scientific talent. Sherry was served and it was soon clear that Fuchs had outdone himself: somehow he had found a vintage of distinction – indeed, it was so good that, contrary to plan, people were soon returning to the bar for a second glass. Despite this, and by some sort of miracle, everyone was not only present but seated at the appointed hour of 8.20 p.m., and dinner was served.

A thick pea soup began the meal; it had arrived from the home of Genia Peierls an hour earlier in metal buckets, but now found its way on to the tables more elegantly in soup bowls, or whatever could be made to pass for soup bowls (the Lodge did not have crockery for 200). For the main course there was a choice: turkey and boiled ham, steak-and-kidney pie or roast beef, all accompanied by potato salad in the British style. Carving the beef was Rudi Peierls, leader of the British team and one of the two men who, five years earlier in Birmingham, had first glimpsed the way in which the bomb could be built. For pudding there was Mrs Moon's trifle, a dish that many of the Americans had never encountered before and which a number did not like – surreptitiously they slid their portions into table drawers, where the sticky mess would be discovered much later. Finally there was port, circulated in the appropriate fashion, to accompany toasts to King George VI, to President Truman and above all to lasting friendship and cooperation between Great Britain and the United States.

The last of the port drunk, the tables were pushed aside and the guests danced a Paul Jones while the stage was prepared for the show. This performance began with a pantomime entitled *Babes in the Wood* which, though billed as 'British-style', had a character all its own. While Titterton played piano and members of the British team, in preposterous costume, went through the motions on stage, a narrator told the story of 'Good Uncles Winnie and Franklin', 'Bad Uncles Adolf and Benito' and the men and women of Los Alamos. This was punctuated by a series of sketches, the most popular of which lampooned the security arrangements on the Hill, by general consent excessive. The ordnance expert James Tuck, personifying security in a red Devil's suit with a flashing light-bulb in the tail, forced a perplexed Philip Moon to eat his own paperwork to ensure it did not fall into the wrong hands. The performance reached its climax with a low-budget re-enactment of the 'Trinity Test', the occasion two months earlier when many of those present had seen the first bomb test-fired in the New Mexico desert. Instead of an atomic weapon on a steel tower, however, this time there was a bucket on a step-ladder, and instead of an electrical impulse to fire it there was a lighted cigarette, tossed nonchalantly into the bucket by George Placzek. Flares, lighting and sound effects did not quite rise to the occasion, but the joke was taken. The show was, recalled one American witness, 'a smash hit'. One of the gruff US Army colonels who ran the camp was seen laughing fit to burst, and he remarked afterwards that it was not true the British had no sense of humour.

There was more. The chairs were now moved again and the dancing began, to music provided in part by gramophone and in part by the incomparable Titterton, the longest-serving British resident on the Hill whose jazz performances on the Lodge piano were already legend. Meanwhile the bar did a roaring trade, although it had been artfully laid out to ensure there was always some congestion in the approaches – 'in this way,' remarked Peierls later, 'the drinks lasted to the end'. Everyone, in fact, had as much to drink as they wished, and some ('the regulars', according to Peierls) had too much. The hall had balconies on two sides, about twelve feet up, and one of the young British scientists who had helped with the lighting began amusing himself by dropping light bulbs on the floor below, to hear them pop. When he narrowly missed Kitty Oppenheimer a senior scientist stepped in and saw him to his bed. The merriment lasted until 3 a.m., when the last guests went reluctantly on their way.

A few days later Peierls reported on the party to his superiors at the British mission in Washington. The taxpayers' $500, he was able to say, had been well spent. 'It seems to have been extremely successful in every respect and our guests repeatedly said that it had been the best party yet on the Hill, which even allowing for some polite overstatement sounds quite good.' One couple, he reported, had gone so far as to say that the event passed off so smoothly and efficiently that it was 'almost American'. And he concluded: 'Perhaps you could also transmit to the Treasury people our appreciation for their generosity.'

Brian Cathcart is the author of *The Case of Stephen Lawrence*. His next book will tell the story of British breakthroughs in atomic science in the 1930s.

TIM LOTT

·················

Frankie's Christmas

CHRISTMAS DAY, TWENTY YEARS AGO. INTERIOR OF FRANKIE'S
CHILDHOOD HOME, FRONT ROOM. FLASHBACK. DAYTIME.

*A child, about eight years old, recognizably Frankie, is looking over the other
side of the street at the lit windows. It is raining.*

P.O.V. terraced houses. Daytime.

The windows reveal scores of Christmas cards, trees, decorations, presents.

P.O.V. Frankie's childhood home, front room. Daytime.

*A few cards. A pathetic Christmas tree. No decorations. A few not very good
presents. His mother, Flossie, and his father, Joe, sit on separate, bare armchairs.
Sound of doorbell.*

*Frankie's father opens the door. A child, recognizably Colin, wearing full
QPR kit, rushes into the room, holding a present for Frankie. Colin's father,
Billy, stands behind him.*

BILLY: Colin!

*He has a Glasgow accent. Colin, obviously frightened, quickly moves back to
the doorway. We see that he has a faint black eye and is pale. His father is
big, thuggish. The implication is obvious.*

JOE: Come in, Billy. Happy Christmas. Happy Christmas, Colin.

*The voice of Joe is soft, friendly, but very quiet. Joe is clearly a shy man, ill at
ease with others. Billy and Colin come in. Billy is staggering slightly. It is clear
that he is drunk.*

COLIN: Dad. Can I . . . ?

Billy nods peremptorily and Colin runs towards Frankie. Frankie's face lights

94

up. Colin hugs him. Frankie, grateful but a little embarrassed and stiff, hugs
him back. Billy and Joe stand next to each other, in silence.

BILLY: Any chance of a wee drop?

JOE: Of course. I'm sorry. We don't usually keep anything in the house,
but I've got something 'of the hard stuff' somewhere, I think. Flossie?

Flossie comes into the room. She also seems quiet and shy. She blushes.

FLOSSIE: Hello, Billy. Happy Christmas.

Billy nods.

JOE: Could you fetch Billy a Scotch. I think there's some in the top
of the larder.

Flossie leaves.

P.O.V. Frankie and Colin.

Colin is busily unwrapping a present from Frankie. It is something cheap and
unimpressive. Colin seems thrilled anyway. Now Frankie opens Colin's present.
It is a beautiful, and obviously very expensive, telescope, which makes Frankie's
gift seem ridiculous.

FRANKIE: Colin, I . . .

COLIN: It's for seeing things better.

Colin takes the telescope from Frankie and looks at him through it.

P.O.V. View through telescope of Frankie.

Out of focus. Colin can't work out how to focus it. Frankie helps him, until
the image is sharp and clear. Frankie appears huge through the telescope.

Interior of front room. Daytime.

Frankie takes the telescope from Colin and fondles it. He clearly thinks
it's wonderful. He reverses it and looks at Colin.

P.O.V. View through telescope of Colin

Colin appears tiny, insignificant, distant. Frankie laughs.

Interior of front room. Daytime.

Joe takes the telescope from Frankie.

JOE: What's this?

BILLY: The boy saved up all year for it. Cost a fortune.

JOE: It's lovely. But we can't accept it. It's too . . . nice. Too expensive.

BILLY: Ah. Go along with you.

FLOSSIE: No. We really couldn't. [*To Colin*] It's lovely, Colin. But it's
... Why don't you take it back to the shop, love, and get something for
yourself, eh? Maybe get Frankie a little something? You understand,
don't you, Frankie?

> *Frankie nods. It's clear that on some level he does understand, that he is
> embarrassed by the lavishness of the gift and that he agrees it should go back.
> He notices that Colin looks somewhat crushed. Billy, meanwhile, is knocking
> back a very large Scotch.*

BILLY: I told you it was stupid.

FRANKIE: Can we play with it for a little while, though?

> *Billy looks sceptical.*

JOE: It's Christmas day, I suppose.

BILLY (*to Colin*): One scratch on that, boy, and you're in hospital.

> *Frankie and Colin run off to the window, thrilled.*

Interior of Frankie's bedroom. Daytime.

> *Frankie's bedroom is covered in QPR posters. He is looking out of his
> window with the telescope that Colin has just given him. Colin stands next
> to him, waiting a turn.*

P.O.V. Windows of House in street opposite.

> *We see through the telescope the happy families and excited children, all in
> marked contrast to the bleakness of the scene at Frankie's house. The telescope
> eventually comes to rest on one window. It is recognizably Nodge, as an
> eight-year-old. His bedroom is covered with QPR posters too. He is dressed
> brightly, flamboyantly, in primary colours, and seems very different to his
> drab, adult self.*

FRANKIE: Who's that?

> *He gives the telescope to Colin, who looks.*

COLIN: His name's Jon Cromwell. He just moved in.

> *He gives the telescope back to Frankie.*

P.O.V. Nodge in his room viewed through the telescope lens.

> *Nodge is surrounded by books, with discarded Christmas wrapping. Annuals,
> encyclopaedias, children's novels. He is reading* The Boy's Book of

Travel. *It shows glamorous foreign landscapes on the cover. Suddenly Nodge looks up, directly at Frankie. He gives a faint smile, as if he can see that he is being watched. Embarrassed, Frankie immediately refocuses the telescope to the street.*

P.O.V. The street.
A man and a woman, Sicilian, beautifully dressed, are walking down the street with a small black dog. Their faces are extremely cruel. By their side, a boy, again about eight, recognizably Diamond Tony. Again, beautifully dressed. He looks innocent, nervous.

FRANKIE: It's that Italian boy. Have you ever spoken to him?

COLIN: He doesn't speak English. He's foreign. My dad says he's a greasy wop.

The Sicilian family walk past two black men. The dog bolts. The Sicilian man shouts something, we do not hear what. The two black men turn suddenly and begin shouting angrily at him. The man gestures back. The black men turn on him, and begin kicking and beating him. The woman screams. Tony just looks very, very frightened, then hopelessly tries to pull one of the men off.

Interior of Frankie's bedroom. Daytime.
Billy walks into the room. He is now very drunk.

BILLY: Come on.

COLIN: But Dad . . .

Colin tries to indicate the scene outside.

BILLY: Don't you answer me back, boy.

He goes to swipe Colin across the face. Frankie stands in his way.

BILLY: Get out of my fucking way.

Frankie doesn't move.

COLIN: It's alright, Frankie. Don't . . .

Frankie still doesn't move. Stalemate. Billy moves a step forward. The door opens and Flossie walks in.

FLOSSIE: Time to be going now, Colin love. Thanks very much for the present. It was a lovely thought. You've got a good boy there, Mr Burden.

BILLY [*viciously*]: He's a wee fucking homosexual. Scuse my language, Flossie. Come on.

Finally, Frankie moves out of the way. Colin moves to the door, holding the telescope. He turns as he goes. Frankie gives him an encouraging smile.

FRANKIE: Happy Christmas, Col.

Colin, obviously grateful, gives Frankie a smile. They leave.

Close on: Frankie's face, looking sad, concerned.

Tim Lott is writing the screenplay of his novel *White City Blue* for BBC Films.

BARRY UNSWORTH

....

From a Notebook

Here in Umbria, in July, the chicory flower comes into its own. Walking around in the middle hours of the day you are hardly aware of them – they close in the heat. But morning and evening they come out and the borders of the roads and edges of the banks are massed with this sudden amazing blue. They avoid scorching, they prosper through the torrid weather, they take over the ground, it makes sense. They have to be rooted out, in spite of their beauty, when they encroach too much. And that makes sense too.

Everything makes sense that we see immediately round us from day to day, within the boundaries of our fences, the lines of cypresses that mark the limits of our land. Just now the vines, in contrast to their reluctant beginnings, are gushing out luxuriantly, reaching high overhead, clutching at the grasses underneath. They have their necessary confines too – we have to tie back the trailing shoots, cut away those too close to the ground. They have to be freed from the random entanglements, the loops of the tendrils have to be uncurled so that the sprays can be fastened more securely to the wires. So thin and delicate, these tendrils, and so tough, so tenacious of life.

Not too fanciful to think that this same recognition of limits, this same control of energy, are what characterized the masons and fresco-painters whose work we see in the medieval hill-top towns that are so much a feature of the Umbrian landscape. Those artists worked within the tranquil confines of the churches, what they did made sense. But when they stepped outside into the light of day they entered a world of plague and famine and incessant war. The churches were built and decorated in one of the worst periods in recorded history for the common people in Europe to be alive.

We for our part have no need to go beyond our fences to enter a world every bit as dangerous and bloody. Voices and faces from that world come on the ether, the silence of this place is charged with them. The smallest of gestures and they are here with us in our living-room, mass graves in Kosovo, starving children and mutilated villagers in Africa, gang killings in the south of Italy, misery and cruelty on an appalling scale. Perhaps we shouldn't switch on? But that would set up fences of a different sort, ones that don't make any sense at all. Not to us at least, in this time and place.

These summer evenings, as the light begins to fade, there is for a while a luminous deepening of colour, the stubble-fields glow, the green of the trees darkens and shines. As though flung upwards into the western sky, small clouds are startled into radiance, still held in the regard of the invisible sun. There is the little wood and stream below, marking the boundary on that side. There is the gate and the fence, the long line of cypresses indicating the precise limits of our territory. And there is a precarious quality in the silence. Why can't we find virtue in detachment, is that only for saints?

Losing Nelson by Barry Unsworth is published by Hamish Hamilton.

ACKNOWLEDGEMENTS

The publishers gratefully acknowledge permission from the following to reprint extracts from work in copyright and to print previously unpublished material:

Martyn Bedford for 'Attaining the VIZ' © Martyn Bedford, 1999. Ronald Blythe for 'From *Out of the Valley*' © Ronald Blythe, 1999. Alain de Botton for 'A Contemporary Love Story' © Alain de Botton, 1999. Brian Cathcart for 'The Bomb Party' © Brian Cathcart, 1999. Helen Dunmore for 'At the Lake' © Helen Dunmore, 1999. Esther Freud for 'It's William's Birthday' © Esther Freud, 1999. Fergal Keane for 'Christmas in Cape Town' © Fergal Keane, 1999, first published in the *Independent*, 2 January 1999. Marian Keyes for 'The Press Launch and the Rules of Engagement' © Marian Keyes, 1999. Matthew Kneale for 'Mesmerizing the Pig' © Matthew Kneale, 1999. Tim Lott for 'Frankie's Christmas' © Tim Lott, 1999. Roger McGough for 'A Serious Poem' © Roger McGough, 1999. Patrick McGrath for 'The Taproom' © Patrick McGrath, 1999. John Mortimer for 'Wheelchairs' © Advanpress Ltd, 1999. Jamie Oliver for 'My Perfect Christmas Pressie' © James Oliver, 1999, illustration copyright © Alex Rusch. Vic Reeves for 'From *Sun Boiled Onions*' © Vic Reeves, 1999. Barbara Trapido for 'Jacopo's Room' © Barbara Trapido, 1999. Barry Unsworth for 'From a Notebook' © Barry Unsworth, 1999. Edith Velmans for 'Good Neighbours' © Edith Velmans, 1999. Simon Winchester for 'The Dubrovnik Peace Project © Simon Winchester, 1999.